T0064632

INTERDIMENSIONAL DANCING

the evolutionary power of spiritual experiences in one's life

DIANE STEPHENSON

Balboa Press books may be ordered through booksellers or by contacting:

Balboa Press
A Division of Hay House
1663 Liberty Drive
Bloomington, IN 47403
www.balboapress.com
1 (877) 407-4847

Print information available on the last page.

ISBN: 978-1-5043-3009-1 (sc)
ISBN: 978-1-5043-3011-4 (hc)
ISBN: 978-1-5043-3010-7 (e)

Library of Congress Control Number: 2015904505

Balboa Press rev. date: 04/03/2015

CONTENTS

PREFACE

Years ago I was told to keep a journal. I heard that message from several sources so I knew it was an important teaching of the time. "We are in a time of change," I was told, "and journaling will be a record of that change for your children and grandchildren to learn from."

I thought it was too boring to write about daily routines and I really did not understand the changing political atmosphere of the time so I did not want to journal about those things. I started a Spiritual Journal instead. I wrote about the extraordinary things that happened in my life that altered my point of view and taught me something. I wrote about the things that actually caused change and evolution to occur in me.

I realized that there are beings in the unseen realms that take an active role in our personal evolution and help us. I was being taught truth from a higher perspective by those beings. I have seen ascended masters in dreams and visions and heard their voices questioning or instructing me. I am no longer surprised when an event like this happens, I look forward to it!

In conversations with friends I would sometimes share one of these experiences and often I would hear in response, "You should write a book!" We are all being guided but, too often, we do not recognize it and we cast it aside as something out of the realm of possibility. I am hoping to bring the reader's attention to the recognition that this is happening to them too. We all have an inner teacher that is trying hard to capture our attention and walk with us on our evolutionary journey!

Your life will improve once you connect to the Higher Power. The boundaries of limiting belief systems will be erased. Mental and emotional problems will dissolve. Creativity will flow and a feeling of freedom will arise.

INTRODUCTION

The inspiration to write this book came from my desire to share my spiritual experiences with my children. Then, the inspiration came to share with all who are affected by unsupportive belief systems and, as a result, struggle to comprehend certain inner states. We seldom hear the voice of Spirit guiding us when we project outward and judge, label, or blame another for our situation or circumstance.

The spiritual part within ourselves is our connection to our Creator and it will teach and guide us in truth. My attentiveness to that part within myself became the focus of my life. Connecting with that part is liberating and I am very liberated by it!

The physical body is created by our parents and our eternal self (our spirit) enters that body at birth. We become whole when we recognize and identify with our spirit. We gain a higher perspective that enables us to see life through different eyes.

The problems we have in the world today are because we have become disconnected from our spirit, our wholeness. Our spiritual self is connected to cosmic consciousness and one of its qualities is all knowledge. When we have access to all knowledge, we have spontaneous right action. Spontaneous right action can only advance the world, not destroy it; can only advance the self, not destroy it.

Drawing our attention to the spiritual part of ourselves is our goal. We are all connected to the Source that sustains us. To become aware of this connection is to become whole. It is simply a process of raising personal vibration from the lower levels of fear, anger, judgment and depression to the higher realms of love, gratitude and appreciation.

Being spiritual and being religious is not the same thing, they are two different experiences.

Spiritual teachers are enlightened masters and some are Gurus. They have reached this state themselves and teach us how to reach this state by overcoming our internal obstacles, fears, limiting belief systems, and other impediments that stand between us and our state of joy and enlightenment. We are their sisters and brothers. We need to do our part and then comes grace.

Once I saw a photo of Paramahansa Yogananda standing out in the cosmos with planets and universes in the process of being born and dying all around him. The caption read To Stand Unafraid Amid Crashing Worlds. I realized this is what I want to do! I want to stand unafraid and unaffected by whatever happens in life. My response, not reactions, will come from my internal state of peace and centeredness.

One time at Mystery School with Joseph Beautiful Painted Arrow in New Mexico, in a flash of "knowing," I realized that the story of Adam and Eve is actually the story of Atom and Evolution. All of creation is in an evolutionary process and planets and universes are in different stages of that process just like people are in different stages of the aging process from the newborn to the dying. Our planet Earth is at a point in evolution where it will graduate to the next level. This means the planet and everything on it is vibrating higher and we humans are now capable of vibrating higher along with the planet. All we need to do is release or cease to resist all the lower vibrating emotional feelings within us.

Negative emotions are simply tightly bound balls of energy that arise from within and, if we cease to engage them and cease to resist them, and instead simply observe them (the spiritual part of us is the observer), they will unwind and dissipate. The energetics of our planet are forcing these emotions to the surface for release. Simply observing them will release them from our inner world, although it may take several times to fully release any deeply seated emotion.

Prayer is another topic that needs clarity. We should not pray as a beggar asking Spirit to please give us this or that. Like attracts like so thanking Spirit for what we already have, even if we feel we do not have enough, will attract more. Prayers do not have to be long, they can be as short as three words, "thank you Spirit" or be expressed in true feelings. Prayers of gratitude increase vibration and bring about more to be grateful for. Every time something happens in my life that others may consider "lucky" I say "thank you" because I know it is not luck, it is synchronicity, and synchronicity is a spiritual quality.

I hope you enjoy reading this book of spiritual experiences. I live in two worlds, the physical world and the spiritual world and what a wonderful adventure it is! These experiences taught me truths I incorporated into my life, and each time I downloaded a new truth, my life became happier and less stressful.

Spirit would appear to me in forms I recognized and understood. The images presented to me were for my comprehension and evolution and may not necessarily be repeatable or applicable to anyone else. Many of the encounters I had were life changing. My life changed, then time marched on and my life changed again and again.

Everyone learns by experience and some people are able to learn from the experience of others. I hope you take something away from this book that enriches your life or helps you on your evolutionary journey.

With love and gratitude.
Diane

THE CANYON ROAD

April 1974

I work at Los Angeles International Airport and live with my family in Thousand Oaks. There are lots of commuters that live in rural communities and drive downtown to work on a daily basis. I carpool with two co-workers but today I am traveling alone. The trip usually takes about an hour. I drive over Malibu Canyon then along Pacific Coast Highway to the airport.

Malibu Canyon is a winding two lane road. About halfway through, there is a tunnel cut through the mountain. As I come out of the tunnel, the road clings to a rock wall on one side and drops off about 300 feet down to the canyon floor on the other side. There is a small stone wall about three feet high that serves as a guard rail and alerts drivers to the drop off. This is the most dangerous section of the road.

This morning, just after I come out of the tunnel, I hear a car engine racing. I look in the rear view mirror and do not see anything. I hear brakes squealing so I look out my side window and see a car driving erratically and coming up alongside me as if to pass. I can hear the engine racing, the brakes screeching, and the front tires are smoking! I instantly know the throttle is stuck open and the car is out of control. Incidents of this type have been reported on the news.

The vehicle lunges toward me so I pull close to the rock wall. Then the car drops back and lunges forward several more times, as if the breaks are working then failing then working and failing again. I hit my brakes and pull as close to the rock wall as I possibly can and stop, hoping that car will pass me. The out of control car then makes an abrupt turn and lunges straight for me!

Everything shifts into slow motion. I know I am going to die. I am going to be crushed up against the side of this rock wall! I peer at the side view mirror knowing it will be the first part of my car to be ripped off from the inevitable impact.

I look up at the driver in the oncoming car. I can see her clearly. She is wide-eyed and fighting the steering wheel all the way. Her arms are outstretched and she is pressed back into her seat, both feet on the brake trying with all her might to stop the vehicle. She also knows what is about to happen. I resign myself to death. I look again at the side mirror, waiting to see it torn off. I watch her closing in on me, she is within inches from me now when her car jumps sideways, reverses direction and goes back across the road! As if an invisible shield is placed between her car and mine! Her car strikes it, bounces back across the road, and lands perfectly balanced atop the three foot stone wall. All four wheels are off the ground, the engine is still racing, the wheels are still spinning, and she is slumped over the steering wheel. I feel as through an act of divine intervention just happened!

I get out of my car and look around. The entire chain of cars behind me is stopped and the drivers are running towards her car suspended there on the small stone wall. There are enough people gathering to help her so I decide to drive to the Sheriff Station at the bottom of the canyon to get help.

My drive to the Sheriff Station is full of gratitude, amazement and reflection. I wonder "who am I" and "what am I going to do in this lifetime that I should be preserved and protected?" It is the first time I realize someone is watching over me and helping me. It feels good!

I know the other car actually struck something that reversed its direction. Not only I was protected, the other driver was also protected. She landed perfectly balanced atop a three foot stone wall, where her engine could race out of control until it ran out of gas and harm no one.

Stop Smoking

1974

I am recently married and my husband wants me to join his church. In order to join, I have to quit smoking, which I do not want to do. So I tell my husband "yes I'll quit smoking" but I really have no intention of quitting. I figure I will just hide it from him. Several weeks go by and I continue to be a secret smoker.

This afternoon I am out in my backyard, secretly smoking, and I feel something wrap around my ankle and leg and pull me down. I try to stand up and it pulls me down again. With all the talk about church and the devil I am hearing lately, I figure it is either the devil or one of his minions reaching up and grabbing me saying, "As long as you smoke you are mine!"

Well that does it! The devil should know better than to touch me! I stand up, pull my leg free, and flick the cigarette directly at him on the ground! "You think you own me because I smoke! You do not own me!" In my mind I am declaring war, a war to set myself free from the chains of hell, and I quit smoking that very minute.

The next day, I find I have to change my whole routine because I have too much time left on my hands and I am nervous. I am used to getting up every morning and making a cup of coffee, sitting at the kitchen counter on my leather bar stool, and smoking while I watch the sun come up.

I need to get up later, I cannot sit at the kitchen counter because it evokes the desire to smoke, and I cannot drink coffee anymore either because it is all part of the "pattern of smoking." I have to change that pattern in order to quit. I become aware of how much time I have spent smoking every day! My day seems so much longer now!

It is the third day and I am beginning to feel dizzy and disoriented. I find myself walking around my house not knowing where I am going or why. I think a Pepsi or a Coke may help me feel better so I drive to McDonalds and forget how to get home. I have to sit in my car and wait for my senses to come back. I cannot work for a week because I am too disoriented.

I begin to have what I would call seizures. Luckily I can feel them coming. They start like a small earthquake inside that shakes my nervous system and then my whole body starts shaking. I am always afraid of losing control at this point. After the first one, I know how they progress so now when I feel one coming I pray, "Dear God, please help me get through this and I promise I will not bother you again, I will stop at a store and buy a pack of cigarettes." After each seizure I think "maybe this will not happen again" and, as a result of that thought, I never do buy another pack of cigarettes. The seizures continue for several weeks. At first I have about six a day and then, day after day, they begin to taper off until they stop. If I happen to be driving and feel one coming, I just pull over to the side of the road and wait it out.

My chest is tightening up. It feels like someone is putting a clamp between my two rib cages then pulling them together. It is very uncomfortable!

After about six months, I decide to see if I am still a smoker. I ask a friend for a cigarette. I light it up, take one drag and feel that same familiar feeling I always feel when I smoke. I know I am still addicted so I put it out immediately!

Every six months or so I light up a cigarette to see if I am still a smoker and every time I get that same familiar feeling. I know I am still addicted so I put the cigarette out and wait for more time to pass.

After three years I light a cigarette and choke on it! It is just like the first time I ever lit one up and choked on it. I am no longer addicted! I feel really good about this! Shortly after, I feel the clamp in my chest release and I feel my chest relax and expand again.

I have talked to a lot people that have quit smoking and most of them say they think about smoking often. Some people even say they think about it all the time. I never think about it! It never enters my mind and I have no desire to smoke. Smoking has been completely removed from me!

Several years later I dream that I am smoking. It takes me some time to realize it is only a dream because it feels so real. Maybe this dream is, or will be, my final experience of ever being a smoker!

I actually never liked smoking in the first place, I just got addicted to it. I worked as a telephone operator for Pacific Bell and everyone smoked in the cafeteria during lunch and breaks. To be part of the group I started smoking. I never enjoyed it. I did not like the way it smelled and I did not like the way it made me smell. I only felt clean after my morning shower and until my first cigarette of the day. The rest of the day I could smell smoke on me and that always made me feel dirty.

My Wake Up Call

1981

My husband and I decide it would be better for our children to raise them in the country so we purchase a small motel and move to a remote little town in Idaho. The motel comes with a three bedroom house that will accommodate our family nicely.

One day, while cleaning one of the rooms, I find a book in the trash can titled Whole Brain Thinking by Jacquelyn Wonder. Reading this book helps me realize how I have been taught to reject half of my own being, my right brain feminine emotional side, and judge it as weak and unstable.

The left side of the brain is masculine, logical, and linear and does not feel emotion. The right side is feminine, intuitive, and creative and feels emotion. This book teaches me how to use both sides of my brain, which is a life-enhancing and a life-altering experience.

Communication from Spirit to its creations is transmitted through light. Light carries information and vibration. Planet Earth and everything upon the planet including plants, animals, minerals, and people receive information and increase in vibration via the light from our Sun and our entire cosmos.

Inspiration or ideas come down as *feminine descending light*. Those inspirations and ideas, when they reach the bottom of their descent, are manifested out into the world by the *masculine horizontal light*.

When the light is received by the feminine, the feminine side says, "How does this feel?" If it feels like a good idea, it gives the idea to the masculine side of the brain for consideration and manifestation. The masculine side weights the possibilities. "What is needed to manifest this?

How will this work? Will it be worth the effort?" After the masculine side figures that out it gives the information back to the feminine side for approval. The feminine side again weights the information. "How does this feel?" (Feeling is a faculty of intuition.) If it feels like a good idea, the feeling of "let's do it" arises. If it feels like "it will not work doing it that way," the feminine gives the idea back to the masculine for re-thinking. This back and forth process continues until the agreement of "let's do it" arises or the agreement of "this is a bad idea, let's discard it" arises. This is Whole Brain Thinking!

Our society has separated men and women and this has reverberated internally into separating ourselves, our emotions from our intellect, to our detriment. Let's not deny our feelings. Let's look at them and consider them, allowing them to be without fighting against them. Accepting who we are, all of who we are, is part of the healing and an evolutionary process.

Whole Brain Thinking stimulated my desire to use all of my brain in guiding my own life and I practiced the visual exercises in the book. This picture is an example of that practice. Focusing attention on the white you see a vase. Focusing attention on the black you see two faces. Switching back and forth between the black and the white stimulates whole brain thinking.

Next, I read a book by Suzanne Somers titled Keeping Secrets, the autobiography of her childhood years growing up with an alcoholic father. She talks about how that experience, and the coping techniques she developed during those years, interfere in her adult relationships. As a child she becomes a "controller" and an "enabler" in order to protect herself and other family members when her father comes home intoxicated.

Keeping Secrets makes me realize I am a BIG TIME enabler in my family so I begin to watch myself and catch myself in the act of being that enabler. I try to control my children so they will not upset their father. My intention is to avoid a family fight and preserve the peace in our home. Being in a controlling mode to establish peace is an issue I share with Suzanne. Her book focuses my awareness on the enabler within me and catapults it into the spotlight of my attention! I resolve to quit being that enabler, which holds patterns in place, and instead allow patterns, and everyone using those patterns, to evolve.

These two books are my wakeup call!

Rapid Eye Technology

1990

We move out of Idaho to Washington state in 1986 and then to Oregon in 1988. Living in Salem we hear about a new therapy being developed called Rapid Eye Therapy. By attending open group meetings we learn more about it.

In 1990, the Rapid Eye Institute opens and my husband enrolls as a student. He wants me to accompany him for moral support and he obtains permission for me to be an observer. I sit in the back of the room during every class.

The school is wonderful! Information is disseminated about the brain and its inner workings along with every other therapy modality out there. There are lots of hands-on training and experiential exercises. The students become a close knit group and many friendships are born.

Near the end of the semester the founder, Ranae Johnson, comes to me and says, "Why don't you participate in the class? You would make a great therapist." I say, "I thought I was only here to provide moral support." She says, "If you want to become a therapist just participate and you can graduate with the rest of the class." I feel honored and I am surprised! I ask if I may attendant the next training session so I can participate from the very beginning of the class. Ranae agrees and I enroll in the next session.

I graduate in 1991, open an office on the ground floor of our home, and my book of business begins to grow.

The State of Oregon enacts rules and regulations that affect my business and the school. The school changes our occupational name from Rapid Eye Therapist to Rapid Eye Technologist. To be a therapist in the

State of Oregon now one needs a Master Degree and many graduates of this school are lay people.

I realize my clients need comfort on occasion and need to feel the human touch on their hand or on their arm. In Oregon it is illegal to touch someone as a Rapid Eye Technician. I decide to become a Reiki practitioner. Reiki practitioners are allowed to touch people.

Clients have issues that come up occasionally that they need to understand and "talk out," however, I cannot council them without a Social Worker's license. I become a minister; ministers are allowed to counsel.

All these wonderful modalities come to me and my book of business continues to grow!

ATTENTION DIVERTERS

1991

Difficulties continue to arise in my personal relationships. Sometimes they overwhelm me and I give up. I feel stuck in the muck of it all, like I am sinking in quicksand, so I withdraw into myself and isolate.

The first time I feel defeat and isolate myself from it all, I hear voices calling to me, "Hey, hey look over here, look over here!" I look toward the voices and I see six pink colored lights, like flashlights, randomly waiving around in the air. They are quite close to me. It seems like they are standing in the same room with me.

In my mind's eye, I see three invisible beings standing in complete darkness. They are all holding flashlights, one in each hand, that emanate a soft pink light. They are calling to me to look at them while frantically waiving their flashlights around in the air to capture my attention. They succeed! They have my attention! They continue to wave the flashlights around while slowly walking backward until they disappear from view. When they are gone, I am no longer sinking in the muck, I am standing on high ground wondering what to do next. They have diverted my attention from the despair that was about to consume me.

Time passes and I fall into despair again and they intervene in exactly the same way. Three beings calling to me while waving flashlights to capture my attention. However, this time they are not as close. They are at least halfway between me and the horizon. It takes them longer to attract my attention and, as before, once they have it they back away until they disappear from view.

I see them again and this time they are standing on the horizon. They are frantically waving their flashlights around in the air! They appear so small and tiny in the distance that I almost do not see them at all! As they back away, they just kind of fall off the horizon, disappear really quickly, and somehow I know I will not see them again.

This thought gives me a bit of a shiver. I realize, that if I sink into despair again, they will not show up to rescue me. They have brought my attention to my own problem and it is up to me to resolve it. They leave me with this realization.

In my mind's eye, I thank them and bid them farewell.

Leaving the Light

August 1991

I am a student in the Rapid Eye Therapy class and, as part of our class exercises, we work on each other, we process each other. Two of the ladies here are working with me and I have a vision during this process.

I see myself in a very large room full of light and full of people. There is a party going on and the party is for me! Everyone is wishing me well and giving me presents. Several people say to me, "Are you sure you want to go?" and I reply, "Yes, yes I want to go!" My arms are full of gifts and I am having a wonderful time feeling very honored and loved.

I am meandering around the room greeting and saying farewell to everyone when an Elder comes up to me and says, "It is time to go now," and I feel a gentle hand on my back as I am escorted over to the door. The door opens, the crowd roars their final fond farewell, and I step out.

Outside, I turn around to discover I am standing on a back porch of sorts. There are several steps leading down into space, open space, into the totality of the universe itself! It is enormous! It is vast! It is black! It is unknown! It is overwhelming! I just stand there and stare at it in total shock, overcome by the vastness and incomprehensibleness of it all.

I can see other planets out there and, way way way over to my left in the far away darkness, there is a tiny little ball of light called Earth. That is where they want me to go! I have never seen "dark" before and it is so unfathomably vast I cannot assimilate it. I do not know how to integrate the reality of darkness!

I change my mind! I no longer want to go! I turn around and try to get back through the door, but the door only opens one way, it only opens to let people out! Somehow, in that moment, I understand that the way back in is to go down into the darkness and come back up and out of it again. The path is circular in one direction only, there is no backwards!

I sit down on the top step resting my chin in my hands and my elbows on my knees and stare out into all that space. I sit there for a very long time! Then it occurs to me that I have sat here for so very long and I do not have to pee and I do not feel hungry, so I do not have to eat! Without any bodily demands to respond to I can just sit here throughout all time and eternity! So that is what I am going to do! I am not going! This thought gives me both great relief and momentary joy.

The very next instant I open my eyes to find myself in the bottom of a very large basket and I am screaming. I am three quarters of the way down to earth! I look up and see how far I am from home, from the light, and I feel a deep pain inside me, the pain of separation!

I have no recollection of how I left the back porch and ended up in this basket, but I am pretty sure I did not go willingly! In that moment I realize I have to go through this earth experience, there is no other way back to the light, and I acquiesce.

The vision ends. It informs me that I am not fully present in my body here on earth because I really do not want to be here on earth.

Not being fully present gives me the ability to sort of stand behind myself and watch what goes on around me without being directly involved. Often I am a witness for others experiences and interactions. For a long time I thought that was my purpose in life, to be a witness for others.

I realize my shyness also comes from not being fully present! It is the feeling of, "I am afraid to be here! It is too big and I do not want to put my feet down on the ground here."

The next day in class, a young lady comes up to me and says, "When did you get here? I have not seen you here before." This is my fourth day in class and she has not noticed I am one of the class members. Not being fully present makes me less noticeable and sometimes even invisible to others!

I embrace the fact that I need to become fully present simply because I am here!

La-La Land

September 1992

I am going to drive to the corner gas station. They have a soda machine and I can get a large soda there for 69 cents.

I am standing inside the office at the soda dispenser filling my cup when I hear the station attendant behind the counter hollering at a Chinese man who is standing at the cash register paying for his gas. "How are you going to pay for the rest of it?!!!" The attendant and the manager are both harassing him repeatedly over a $1.95 error.

The Chinese man does not speak English very well. They have misunderstood him and pumped $2.00 too much gas into his car. They are threatening to call the police and charge him with gas theft. The Chinese man becomes very alarmed once he comprehends the threat.

He goes outside, walks around in circles for a few minutes, and then heads toward his car. I can tell he is confused about what to do. Since he does not have the money to pay, he is panicking and deciding to drive away.

I take what I have out of my wallet, intercept him before he reaches his car, and hand him $2.00. He looks at the money, and then at me. I can tell from the questioning look on his face he does not understand, so I gently tug on his upper arm, as if to turn him around, and point towards the office and say, "Go pay, go pay." It takes him a few seconds to figure out what I mean before he turns and walks toward the office.

I do not want the Chinese man to drive away thinking the police will be looking for him, that is why I am giving the money to him to pay instead of paying the attendant myself.

I walk over to my car and then look towards the office to see if he is inside paying. The Chinese man is standing by the office door waiting to catch my attention. He bows to me as a way of saying, "thank you," and I bow to him as a way of replying, "you are welcome." As he turns and enters the office, I get into my car and drive off.

I exit the gas station and enter the street. All of a sudden everything in my vision becomes very illusionary and unreal! The street, stoplight and all the cars morph into black and white cartoon characters! I have entered la-la land!

Everything appears as a black line drawing on white paper. Even my car appears to be a cartoon drawing with big round fenders like a 1940 Ford. I know I am in la-la land and I better be careful! If I bump into one of these other cartoon cars out here on cartoon road, when I come out of la-la land there will be real dents and real insurance claims.

I have to turn left at the stoplight and I am not sure all the cartoon cars I see on the road are all the cars that are really on the road! Will there be cars in the white spaces between the cartoon cars that I cannot see? I decide to take a chance and I turn left in-between two cartoon cars. I make it safely around the corner!

Immediately after turning, I pull to the side of the road and just sit here waiting for la-la land to disappear. Within a few minutes everything becomes normal and familiar again, so I continue on home.

Hanna Barbara and Looney Tunes have made hundreds, maybe even thousands of cartoons. Radio waves circle the earth so video waves probably circle the earth too. Is there a cartoon dimension out there? As a matter of fact, I am pretty sure there is because I accidentally drove through it today on my way home from the gas station.

The Rock

1993

The turmoil I feel inside continues and my head is spinning from it all. Over and over, my mind keeps reiterating arguments and condemnations. I seek relief so I am going to spend a little time with Mother Nature! She always helps me to feel better!

I am driving up the mountain pass and I see a sign for a public campground alongside the Santiam River. I pull in. There is no one here! Summer is over and all the campers are gone!

I find a nice shady spot to park near the river. I lower my car window a little so I can hear the sounds of the river flowing by. I recline my car seat, close my eyes, and start repeating to myself, "I am a rock, I am a rock, I am a rock." Rocks are very still and I imagine they do not think and that is exactly what I want to do right now, stop thinking!

My mind quiets down and everything becomes still. I cannot feel my body anymore and I am at peace! I am in the beautiful space of quiet nothingness when, all of a sudden, in my mind's eye, I see this giant ant walk past me! I realize I really am a rock! I projected my consciousness into a rock! However, judging from the size of the ant that just walked by, I would say I am most likely a tiny little pebble and not a rock!

What is it like to be a rock? I have no feelings, no thoughts, the stillness is pervasive, and the inability to move is something I have never experienced before. It seems that only my ability to "see" is still working and my vision is limited to seeing only what is directly in front of me. I can see blades of grass moving in the breeze, but I cannot feel the breeze itself passing over the surface of the rock.

I am not really a rock, I am still me inside a rock. I am aware of my presence and consciousness while sitting inside this rock.

A Visit to Hell

June 25, 1994

The issue of betrayal is an active component in my life. Because I have experienced this before I want to deal with it fully, so not to experience it again. I must have more lessons around this issue that I need to learn.

I know that I have a part in this and the only thing I have control over is my part. I need to find out what it is "about me" that attracts betrayal and clear it out so I can live in harmony. This is a very painful experience for me.

Feeling betrayed and all the physical discomforts that come with that feeling are present in me. I feel like I am boiling inside, I am sweating profusely and I need to process this. The timing is perfect because I am alone in the house right now. I sit down on the floor with my back resting against my bed, I focus on my feelings, and I let them intensify.

I pray, "Spirit, please help me clear this. Take me down into the heart of the matter and I willingly offer to suffer or go through whatever I need to do to release this. If I have a debt to pay, let me pay it now."

Instantly, I find myself in what religions call "hell." I see huge coals pulsing and emanating unimaginable heat all around me. The coals are the size of giant boulders. It is agonizing being here; it is so intense I cannot even think. The very moment I am to be consumed, Spirit pulls me out and I am back in my bedroom on the floor.

I hear a voice say, "Why don't you kill yourself? Go hang yourself on that big Sycamore tree in your back yard." I reply, "No, I cannot terrify the neighborhood or my children with a sight like that!" Then the voice says, "Drive your car headlong into one of those cherry trees along your driveway." I say, "No, I need to leave my car to my daughter, not wreck it." Then the voice says, "Shoot yourself in the laundry room, you know where the gun is." I reply, "No, I will not leave a mess like that for my family to clean up!" and the voice goes away.

Again I pray, "If there is more to this debt that I owe, I want to pay full measure for it now!" and I find myself right back in among the coals, suffering right up to the point of extinction, when Spirit pull me out again.

My head feels as though it will split open and I am gasping for air. I ask, "Spirit, is there anyone, a friend, who can come and guide me out? I go with people into their personal hell all the time and guide them out when I do therapy with them."

Spirit responds, "There are no friends who can go with you into hell just to remind you how to get out. They are all afraid of it. Only those cloaked in love can enter hell and come out unscathed. Then the pain there does not touch you."

I respond, "Isn't there an ascended master who can come and guide me out? Isn't there someone who can come and help me?" And boom!!! I find myself right back in the searing heat again!

I see a dark shadowy figure float towards me. It looks like the outline of a human filled with dark smoke. It is approaching and extending me a hand. I have been taught dark figures are evil and not to deal with them, but then I am already in hell so what could possibly be worse than this!? I reach out and take the figure's hand and instantly I know who it is! It is me! It is me coming to save me!

Suddenly I am back on the bedroom floor, amazed by the teaching! I have to save myself! The energy in the room is completely changed! This experience is over! They have shown me the lesson I need to learn! I have to save myself!

This brings up questions about Jesus. I was taught that Jesus is everybody's savior so why do I have to save myself?

This experience sent me in a new direction. I have to discover how to save myself and not depend on outside help; not the ascended masters and not Jesus. The ascended masters and Jesus teach us how to save ourselves, they do not save us. They can intervene and help us, but we must do the work and save ourselves.

The Death of Diane

February 23, 1995

I am staffing a Rapid Eye training this week and having a difficult time staying present.

I have been feeling detached, like I am floating out in space without any points of reference. Nothing seems to matter and I do not seem to care about anything. Life seems to be a NO-THING. It has no meaning or purpose for me; I came from nothing and I am going back to nothing.

I have been in this space for several weeks. I feel very ungrounded, as though I am floating away.

February 24, 1995

1/3 Part of me is dying
1/3 Part of me is grieving
1/3 Part of me is present

I have to leave the Rapid Eye class for a little while because the part of me that is grieving comes forward and overwhelms the rest of me and I cry. I take the grieving part by the hand and say, "Come with me into this back room, sit in this chair, and go ahead and grieve." (I have created a space in the back of my mind where the grieving part can sit and grieve.) Then I return to class and I can stay present.

Again the grieving part comes forward and overwhelms me to tears. Again I take her by the hand and lead her to the back room, which is similar to a funeral parlor's viewing room, and sit her down on the chair and ask her to stay there and grieve. I see the part of me that is dying laying on a marble slab; she sits up, looks at both of us and lays down again. I leave the two of them there together and go back to my class.

During break, one of the other participants tells me I am dying. She says her husband died recently and his chakras began to spin out and fill the room with his energy; when they completely spun all his energy out, he passed. She told me my chakras are spinning out and that I need to do something about it.

Not really knowing what to do, I think maybe getting grounded will help me feel better. I drive up to Breitenbush Hot Springs and dunk myself in the hot tub and then the cold tub over and over again and it does not make any difference! I just feel heavier and heavier as the day goes on and my head feels like it is full of fog. By the time I head for home my limbs are so heavy I can hardly move them.

When I get home, I lay down on my bed and say, "Ok! If you want to die go ahead and die!!!"

I close my eyes and create a funeral in my mind's eye for the part of me that is dying. I realize the dying part wants to be honored on her way out so I invite mourners and wailers. About 5 women dressed in black show up howling and carrying on like I have never seen before! They have their arms up in the air and are swaying back and forth as they moan and groan as loudly as they can. The part of me that is laying on the marble slab sits up, looks at the wailers, and lays down again.

The part that is grieving sits in a chair next to her as she lay on her marble slab, and the part that is present invites everyone she ever knew to come here. "Everyone who ever knew me in this lifetime or any other lifetime, you are invited to attend this wake!" The room all of a sudden is full of people! There are mourners and wailers, flowers, guests, even a preacher and it is a grand celebration! The guests are laughing, drinking, and toasting! There is a lot of commotion, noise, and gaiety in the room!

The part that is dying sits up again, looks around at everyone, and lays back down on the slab. A vibration begins inside me and keeps rising higher and higher! I give permission again for the dying part to go ahead and die if she wants to die, it is ok!!!

At this point, I feel a marked separation within me, the physical present me that is laying here on my bed in my bedroom. It feels like a balloon deflating inside me and it's shaking itself loose from my bodily frame. Then I see the top of my head and there is a symbol there, like the flower of life pattern, and the part of me that is dead passes through it escorted by a "spark of consciousness." It passes through, like smoke through a screen door without any resistance, out the top of my head.

I am simultaneously the observer watching from the ceiling and in the physical body lying on the bed watching the dead part leave. The spark of consciousness escorting the dead part looks like an ember, it is glowing a bright red-orange color like a tiny spark from a fire.

As soon as the dead part clears my head, a new energy enters in a swirling motion. It looks like a small white tornado! It swirls down to my feet and screws me into the ground. I am finally grounded!

I open my eyes and it is over! I am wide-awake and ready to start life anew! The dead part has left and a new part has arrived!

It is amazing how resistance to a mental or emotional process can drag that process on for such long periods of time when in the moment of surrender it is over almost instantly.

The Blue Beings

June 1995

I am a licensed practicing Rapid Eye Technician and I have two clients that I have not been able to help. They are both dealing with the same issue, sex addiction. I use every technique available to me and still their issue persists, so I decide to pray about it. I pray for guidance and inspiration to know what to do for these people, as they keep returning for therapy seeking resolution.

In the middle of the night, I wake up vibrating from the high energy in my bedroom. Suspended in the air, somewhere around the ceiling, are three bright blue beings. I cannot determine their size because there is nothing to compare them with; they seem to be beyond time and space. They are a beautiful cobalt blue light, but not emanating the light, they are the light. If you imagine a candle glow without any flame causing the glow, that is what I see.

I float up out of my body and join them at the ceiling. They communicate to me that they are sent in answer to my prayer and say, "Come with us." They tell me everything I need to know to heal my clients as we travel together out into space. I look back at earth and notice we are really far out and I ask, "Where are we going?" They reply, "We are going to the outermost region of your clients' auras." I keep looking back at earth amazed at how far we are from it. I am also amazed that a person's aura is this far reaching!

When we arrive at the outermost region of the first aura, they explain that there is a tear in the subtlest edge of this aura, and the light that enters through the tear becomes distorted, traveling down and manifesting out as behavior. The behavior problem my clients experience cannot be fixed within the mental or emotional bodies; it needs to be fixed at its source, the tear in their aura.

Together we repair the tears in both auras. I am told my clients will need to be patient because the distorted light that is already in their aura will continue its downward journey through all the subtle bodies, and continue to manifest out as behavior. There is no way to remove that distortion, it simply has to pass through and, once it passes, the clear light will follow. Once the clear light reaches their mental and emotional bodies, my clients will then be able to change their behavior. They will then have clear choice and not distortion.

The blue beings bring me back to my bedroom and I thank them. I see my body lying on my bed and, as I float down towards it, I kept repeating, "I am going to remember, I am going to remember, I am going to remember." As I enter my body, I see the wisdom and knowledge imparted to me being extracted out of my head! It looks like an invisible cosmic vacuum is sucking it out!

I find myself awake and fully aware that the knowledge I just received is gone! It is as if I do not have a base within my 3D linear mind for this type of knowledge to land on, so it returns to its source. I have full memory of what happened, but no memory of how to repair a torn aura.

A Dream Fulfilled

1996

Just after the start of the New Year, I leave my marriage with all of its drama behind! I am keeping my eyes open for new opportunities that will appear in my life!

I dream there is a terrible earthquake and all the roads are broken, with pieces of asphalt sticking up in various directions. Travel by car is impossible, so access to medical help for those that are injured is cut off.

I think about this dream for weeks, wondering how to prepare for an event such as this? I surmise a bicycle will be a good alternative source of transportation. It is reliable, does not need fuel, and does not need a road to travel on. I also think about how medical needs for my family and friends might be met if any of them become sick or injured. I wish I knew more about herbs.

I am at Walmart and I notice they are having a drawing for a bicycle. I fill out a card and drop it in the box and ask, "When will the drawing be?" "In about 10 minutes" they reply, so I wait around. I visualize my card being drawn out of the box the whole time I am waiting.

The time comes for the drawing; they shake the box, pull out a card and the announcer takes the card and reads off the name, DIANE STEPHENSON! I win the bicycle! I can hardly believe it!

Shortly after that, a friend of mine decides to open a herb store. The alternative health industry is growing by leaps and bounds and he feels it would be a profitable business. He asks me if I have any interest in becoming his staff herbalist? Of course I say, "Yes, I would love that!" The next semester I enroll in herb school. My friend sponsors my tuition and books while I dedicate all my time and talents to studying and learning about herbs and their healing properties.

One of our class assignments is to go out and find plants in the wild to identify. I am walking near a river in the Oregon Coast Range when I notice the river bank is covered in tiny green plants that are in bloom. They have tiny white flowers that look like stars. They are beautiful and I stop and admire them for a few minutes. I have never noticed that ground cover before and I begin to wonder "what is it? It looks like a sea of stars!"

As I am standing there, I begin to hear a little song in my head that starts out "sea of stars, sea of stars, sea of stars." Then the words melt together and become "stellaria, stellaria, stellaria." I begin to wonder if stellaria is actually a plant name in my Field Guide so I look it up. There it is! Stellaria media, common name chickweed! I am amazed! The photo is a river bank exactly like the one I am looking at and the name of the ground cover is Stellaria media. These plants sang to me their botanical name! How does a plant know its botanical name?

My friend never opened his herb store, but I still have my herbal knowledge and use it to help my family and friends!

The following year, I am at Breitenbush Hot Springs for a three day herbal retreat. In one of the classes the teacher passes around a root and we all take a small piece and chew it. She does not tell us anything about the plant; we are to gather information from the plant as we meditate with it. I ask the plant its name and in a firm deep male voice I hear the word "CELERY!" During discussion later that day; we learn the plant is Osha and its common family name is celery!

I think it is just amazing that both the bicycle and herb school manifested for me out of my dream! And even more amazing that plants can talk and they know who they are, they know their name!

STARGATE MEDITATIONS

SUN & EARTH ENERGY

1997

I meditate with an internet group on a regular basis. We focus on clearing imbalanced earth energies. We all focus on the same intention for each meditation and this meditation's intention is to Re-align the Ring of Fire.

I start the meditation sitting in a chair in my back yard. I imagine a triangle between Catalina Island, the Aleutian Islands, and Hawaii. A triangle pointing to my right comes into my view, then the triangle lights up and changes both shape and directions. It is now an isosceles triangle pointing north.

I can feel movement beneath me. It feels like I am standing on a circular disk that is slowly rotating. I can hear something approaching. I can feel a vibration. There is a beam of light coming down from above and I rotate into it. I am in the center of a strong beam of white light! The disk continues rotating and I move out of the light and into a neutral space.

I hear something approaching again and a few moments later I can feel its vibration, soft and gentle. The energy is coming up from below. It is cool and it reminds me of a leaf. I am in the center of a huge red maple leaf! The disk continues rotating and I move out of the leaf energy into another neutral space.

Around and around I go! Rotating in and out of the light and the dark energy, balancing the warm Sun light from above and the cool Earth energy from below. Soon the meditation is over.

The Four Races

The next meditation brings another very interesting experience. I am shown the original four races on Earth in their original purity. An individual from each race passes in front of me and then moves on, all except the last one. She is African. She stops and lets me look at her for a long time.

She is absolutely stunning! Her hair is pulled back and adorned with bones and feathers and other objects from nature. She is bare-chested and wearing multiple strings of beads made of gold, gems, stones, and other precious minerals from the earth that cover her neck down to her breasts. I can see huge green leaves in the environment behind her and I can hear multitudes of birds chirping all around. She is Royal, the Chief's wife, daughter, or maybe even the Chief herself! She is ageless. She could be anywhere between the ages of 12 and 60!

The most unusual thing about her appearance is her eyes. They are dark in color, clear as crystal, and round, not almond shaped like our eyes are today.

She pauses in front of me for a long time. I can see her breathing and occasionally blinking. I can see her natural motion as she moves ever so slightly. She is observing me as I am observing her. Everything about her is natural. She is of the land and of her village. She fades from view and the meditation ends.

HAWAII

June 1997

Several people from my Stargate meditation group are going to Maui to link up with Ronna Herman's group and I decide to join them. Ronna channels Archangel Michael and she is leading a celebration ceremony for the 10 year anniversary of the Harmonic Convergence.

Around 200 of us are here on Maui for the ceremony. We are standing atop Mt. Haleakala, the volcano, waiting for the sun to rise. The moon is still visible in the west just above the horizon. As the sun rises, I face the sea and stretch out my arms and cup the sun in the palm of my left hand and the moon in the palm of my right hand. The moon hand is freezing cold and the sun hand is extremely hot! This is surprising!

Following Ronna's directions, we all tone to ground the incoming energies. I feel something like a bolt of lightning shoot through me! It goes in my head and out my base chakra into the earth. Metaphorically, it feels like Archangel Michael is running his sword through me! My energy spikes up! I feel stronger and can hold more energy and more light. Something in me has been opened! Shortly thereafter Ronna announces, "It is done!" and we all stop toning.

Up in the sky, directly above me, is the head and face of who I think is an ancient master, maybe Mongolian. He has squinty eyes, a sparse scraggly beard and a fur cap on his head like those they wear in very cold countries. He is very joyous and laughing with glee! I cannot hear any sound but I can see his head moving up and down as he laughs and laughs.

Ronna announces, "The Masters have passed the staff to us. We are to do the work here on the earth now. They are joyous it is accomplished."

I realize that I can contribute to healing everyone on Planet Earth by grounding energy into the core to raise the vibration of the planet. Everybody who walks on this planet absorbs energy through the soles of their feet and, as the vibration from the core increases, each person can absorb that higher energy. I can work with the planet and affect all living instead of working one on one with people, like I do with Rapid Eye Technology. I really like this idea.

I start doing daily grounding meditations. I open my crown and imagine golden light flowing in, through my core, and out my base chakra into the earth. Over time I discover this practice is healing me in the process! As the energy flows through me, it takes problems and concerns out with it. I end each meditation by contributing my love of nature to the flow. I want mother earth to receive not only my negative energy, but my positive energy as well.

Down to Nothing

July 1997

I have a very vivid dream; in fact, it is not a dream. I am actually there! I have to climb over a wooden fence and walk through a corral that is knee deep with wet manure, "in order to get my life back".

This is an uphill climb and, at the top of the slope, there is a long table with several men sitting behind it. There is a book laying on the table, with its pages blowing in the breeze. I am told the book is the "book of my life" and, if I want my life back, I have to climb up the manure-covered slope to retrieve it.

For some unknown reason, I have to take off all my clothes to climb up the slope. So naked, I walk up the slope and, when I get to the top, the table is bare, the men are gone, and my book of life is gone too! I stand there and stare at the empty table for a while befuddled.

I am very upset because they have taken my life and left me with nothing! I walk a few steps down the hill and then stop to consider, "What should I do now?"

I look back up the slope and, to my right, I see a large tree with people merrily skipping around the base of it. I hear a voice say, "Do you want to join them?" I reply, "No, I do not want to spend eternity with those idiots skipping around in a fairy ring!" I have the distinct impression this fairy ring is a place out of time and out of the process of evolution. I do not want to escape my situation, I want to resolve it.

I stand there naked in manure reaching mid-calf, with no life and nowhere to go. I ask myself, "Do I have any options?" I look down inside myself and realize "I still have me!" They can take everything, but they cannot take the me that I am. I am still here!

With the feeling of "I exist" and certainty that nobody can take that away, I walk down the hill to the edge of the manure-covered slope and climb through the rails of the wooden fence into a beautiful green meadow.

Someone is standing there on the other side of the fence to meet me! He speaks to me, but I do not recall the conversation. He guides me over to a beautiful clear stream where I wash the manure off and receive fresh clothes.

Upon awakening, my whole life seems changed. I feel totally alone and do not care about anything. I feel disconnected from my life and I am not sure of my place in the world anymore. I no longer feel like a mother, wife, sister, or friend to anyone! This is a new beginning, and I have to start over with all my relationships.

I feel strange for several days afterward.

Burst into Flames

Spring 1998

I become totally enraged this evening because everything I see in this world is corrupt! I do not want to live here anymore! I do not want to reincarnate and go through this experience ever again! The only way to stop reincarnation is to become a Master, a level I have no chance of achieving in this lifetime. I want to put the "light that I am" out.

I step outside and I stand on the back patio engulfed in rage and, before me suspended in the air, I see myself sitting cross-legged bursting into flames! I am so angry I am self-combusting! Behind the burning me, I see another me and another me and another me, clear back to the first me, the first time this ever happened to me.

My "motherhood" is not honored by men! Men are the co-creators of motherhood, but they do not honor it! If I cannot take care of my children and raise them in love, if I can be overpowered and have to watch my children be dishonored or abused, then I do not want to be here! This is a corrupt, rotten, rigged game and I do not want to play!

I look down the line of me's, sitting behind the burning me suspended there in the air, and there are 100s of them! This has happened over and over and over again! They go clear back to the horizon, each one getting smaller and smaller, back to the first time it ever happened. Each incident building upon the one before until I am completely engulfed in rage and burst into flames!

I sit down with my back against a wall so nobody can sneak up behind me. I fix my eyes on a single point in-between a group of stars and, without blinking or moving, I intend to leave my body. I have no intention of killing myself, I am simply going to exit my body through my head and fly up to the stars.

The stars begin to rotate, one group clockwise and the other group counterclockwise, creating an opening. I am doing it! I am leaving!

Suddenly, a gentle breeze rushes over the fence, surrounds me, and begins to caress me. It feels like a gentle spring rain showering down on me! This lasts for a long time. Slowly, drop by drop, the invisible rain puts out the flames, extinguishes the anger, eliminates the rage that propels me, and pulls me back from the stars!

Then just as suddenly, I find myself sitting alone in the dark and a freezing cold wind rushes over the fence, chilling me to my core! It is over; it leaves me here empty, and I am shaking with cold.

I am thwarted! I am not allowed to leave this planet! Overpowered again! I am stuck here surrounded by corruption. I am incredibly disappointed! I walk back into the house and go to bed.

The next morning I feel empty. I have no feelings about anything. I feel like I have no life and my children are not really my children. This emptiness is hard to bear.

Sacred Postures

1998 - 2000

Judith Thompson leads sacred drumming circles and occasionally stances, also known as sacred postures. There is always a feeling of power, upliftment, and joy in Judith's ceremonies, but I particularly love the stances.

We hold a specific body posture while Judith rattles her bear claw rattle to call in the Spirit of that stance. We "follow the sound of the rattle" with our attention. Merging with the Spirit of the stance is an extraordinary experience that expands our consciousness. Judith never tells us the name of the stance, we discover that when the spirit of the stance comes over us.

My first experience:

The posture for this stance is standing with your head back, mouth open, feet together, and arms at the side while Judith rattles.

My legs are swollen and sore just above my ankles. It is difficult for me to hold this posture because of the discomfort.

Suddenly, the blockage in my lower legs releases, like a flushing toilet, and smoke comes out of my mouth (figuratively). I am a pipe and Mother Earth is smoking me! What a great joy and freedom I feel! She takes about three puffs and I can feel the smoke curling as it comes out of my mouth.

The pipe stance teaches me the sacredness of Mother Earth, that we are connected to her and she has influence in our lives. In this sacred ceremony she honors me by smoking me. In the smoking, she clears the energy blockage in my lower legs.

My second experience:

I am standing with my legs bent, hands in a cupped position over my heart while Judith rattles.

The Spirit of the bear comes over me. I am inside the bear looking out the bear's eyes. I can feel the great strength in the bear's thighs and I can feel the bow of the thighbone itself.

We are walking in a meadow heading towards the woods. We stand on our hind legs and survey the tree line in the distance. I can feel our front paws drooping as we stand on our hind legs looking. We instinctually select an entry point, drop down on all fours, and begin walking towards that point.

We are not hungry, so no instinct to obtain food is present. Inside our head is complete silence! There is no ego! No mind chatter!

This is my first experience of what living without mind chatter and without ego must be like. The bear has no contemplation of thoughts, just instinctual presence.

The bear stance teaches me what great strength feels like and what it is like to be without an ego, without judgment, and without guilt.

My last experience:

We are laying on the ground on our stomachs, foreheads touching the floor, arms at our sides, drums on our backs as rattling begins.

I feel myself digging underground and I begin to become very claustrophobic. It is difficult to breath and I am getting panicky! Then I hear a voice in my head say, "Just dig a little wider" so I do. I dig a wider tunnel and the claustrophobia goes away. I wonder what am I and what am I doing?

Suddenly, I am above ground and looking around. I see a whole group of prairie dogs looking at me! None of the prairie dogs run away so I must be a prairie dog too! I must be part of this big prairie dog community!

The prairie dog teaches me what it feels like to be part of a community and to look out for one another. Being part of a community and feeling accepted is a wonderful feeling!

The Snake

I am laying on the sofa in my living room thinking about cell regeneration and renewal when the image of a snake comes to mind. I wonder, how does a snake renew its skin?

Then I see this huge rattlesnake skin sliding over the top of me! I am inside the snake as it is crawling out of its skin! I ask, "How does the snake do this?"

I can feel the snake concentrating all of its life force energy in its core. This separates the inside from the outside, it shrinks within so to speak. Then it simply slides out of its old skin.

When I have experiences like these I gain understandings that help fortify me in life. This is Spirit and Nature dancing together! Spiritual experiences explain how nature works in the absence of human interference.

Santiam Park

1998 – 1999

There are several parks and campgrounds along the Santiam River in Oregon. I live alone in an apartment and I enjoy spending time outdoors, so I often go and spend time in one of the parks on weekends.

There is one park in particular that I like. It is a very small community park, has about six picnic areas with fire pits, a couple of sports fields, an overnight camping area, and a nice bathroom facility with flushing toilets.

Fall

I drive up to the park, and on the way up, I am wishing I had brought along some wood to start a campfire. It is a little cool today and a campfire would be wonderful.

I stop at a convenience store, purchase a snack, then enter the park. What a wonderful surprise! There is no one at all in the park and there is a raging campfire in one of the picnic areas with a small pile of wood nearby to keep it going! I feel like this is a gift from Spirit just for me!

I setup my chair near the fire and begin to read the book I brought along. The sounds of the flowing river are mesmerizing. I lay my book down and close my eyes. Within a few minutes I can feel the wind blowing through me! I can feel it blowing around every cell in my body! It is a wonderful feeling! Kissed by the breeze! Mother Nature is acknowledging me. I appreciate the magic that happens in this park!

Spring

It is early spring and it is warm enough for me to visit the park again today. The air is still crisp and the sun is warm! Again, no one is here but me! I walk around the park's sport fields for a little exercise, read my book for a while, then decide to rest. The ground is wet so I lay down on top of a picnic table in full sun.

The sun warms my body. The temperature between the sun and the air is absolutely perfect. It is so perfect that eventually, I cannot feel my body anymore. Then I see a light in my inner eye. In that light, I see a whole stream of symbols flow in through my forehead. I can see the symbols as the pass by my eyes on their way downstream. They flow in like a river. Some of them are familiar but most of them are not. There are hundreds of them!

I muse, "So this is what Sun Worshippers do. They are not really worshipping the sun, they are taking in information from the sun!"

I lay there a little while longer, letting my body balance all that sun energy, until I again become aware of the hard table under me and the cool air around me. It is time to get up and head home.

THE GRID EXPERIENCE

March 20, 1999 - The Equinox

I am part of an internet meditation group and I have spoken about them before. I have participated with this group in meditations known as Stargates since 1996. Chandara, our meditation facilitator, receives information via channeling from a group who call themselves The Ancient of Days. She travels around the world to different power spots, opening portals and grounding cosmic energy into the planet. As a group of synchronistic meditators, we are notified via email, and we all meditate with her. We remain in our own physical locations, meditating on the same intention.

In preparation for this meditation, I check the Internet to find out what time it will be here in Salem, Oregon when it is 12:00 noon in St. Petersburg, Russia on March 20, 1999. The intention is to ground the energy of Equality & Balance for All to replace Communism. I need to begin my meditation at 1:00 A.M. to be in synchronicity with the group. At about 12:15 A.M. I light incense, bless my room with Reiki symbols, and wait for the meditation to begin.

Around 12:30 A.M. what feels like a huge swarm of bees enters through the bottoms of my feet and moves up my legs. I close my eyes and begin to meditate knowing the energy is arriving. I circle my breath from my midsection down my right leg, through the core of Mother Earth, back up my left leg, crossing over my midsection, up and out my right arm, across the Christ Grid, back down my left arm, crossing over my midsection, and back down into Mother Earth again continuing this figure eight pattern.

Suddenly I feel a "finger of light" gently touch the top of my head and begin to spin my crown chakra very, very slowly for a very, very long time. I can feel the invisible finger moving through my hair. The color red fills my inner sight and I hear a whirling sound, like helicopter blades hacking the air. I ask for the vibration to increase 3x3x3 and it increases immediately. The sound gets louder and the energy coming into me increases. Everything becomes more intense. The helicopter blade turns sideways and chops my head into neat little slices, like a loaf of bread. Then my head crumbles to my shoulders. A puff of air blows the crumbs away and I wonder, "Maybe this is not Stargate energy, maybe I should discern this."

Immediately the color changes from red to turquoise green and I notice two beings standing one on each side of me. I look up at them and see that they have human bodies and dog heads, with long snouts. They are about eight feet tall and are holding a staff. I can see their chests rise and fall as they breathe. A feeling of fear starts to arise in me. I look at the beings but they never turn their heads to look at me. A thought occurs that this is the origin of the words "watch dog" and "dog soldier." I feel they are here on duty and nothing more, so a feeling of safety starts coming over me and I relax.

We start spinning and rising! I look down and see the Sphinx, the Great Pyramid, and what I think is a cat, golden in color and flattened, like road kill. There is also a large black rectangle that I cannot identify. It is not on any map of Egypt that I have ever seen. It might be an underground structure or an invisible building above ground but, somehow, I can see it.

The vibration in my body amps up every time something new happens. The "dog soldiers" disappear and, all of a sudden, I am a beam of light. The beam expands beyond me and I am in the beam of light. Then, just as instantly, I am inside a multi-faceted double-terminated clear quartz crystal. The flow of energy is tremendous, I have trouble breathing and holding the energy at the same time.

I realize I am part of the Earth's gird system! I am one little segment in it. The whole grid wobbles and I know that, when another group of people join up with the rest of us, we are supposed to stabilize the energy and hold the grid intact. My breath is the key to stabilizing. If I hold my breath, the energy backs up in my solar plexus and I feel as if I am about to explode. I have to keep breathing energy in and exhaling it back out through the grid. The energy increases again, the color in my head turns violet and we all have to work at stabilizing the wobbling grid!

A few minutes later I hear a roar like a rocket approaching overhead! I open my eyes: I am still sitting on my sofa in my living room popping up and down like a popcorn kernel in a hot pan. Tears are streaming down my face. My solar plexus is pulsing in and out like a drum. This is so incredibly intense!

I close my eyes. I am struck in the crown chakra with what feels like a lightning bolt, sending everything into warp speed. The color in my inner sight bursts into brilliant white light and every cell in my body is blown open to let the energy flow through. There is a small white light pyramid spinning inside my head and a large one spinning around my body. I see and feel every chakra on my body spinning. All my cells are engaged in what feels like a cosmic organism. Enormous amounts of electricity are running through my body! I feel like a flag hanging on a pole out in the universe flapping back and forth in the cosmic breeze!

At some point during this experience I contribute three attributes to the grid: Honesty, Integrity, and Acceptance.

Needless to say my whole life changes after this. I am amazed at how much the physical body can feel! My anger and resentments are gone, blown away by the cosmic wind. My negative emotions are replaced by this high electrical charge. In an instant, I am a new person. I am very, very grateful for this experience and for the new life it brings me.

I think this grid construction is something I contracted to do before I was born here on earth. I have heard several channelers say they were just meditating when in pops this entity that says, "Hey, it's time to get together now and channel" and the channeler resists. The entity reminds the channeler they agreed to do this before they were born and now is the time to start. So I think this is something I agreed to do and, when it was time, the dog soldiers came to get me so that I could do my part. Now, unlike the channelers, my part is done.

The Purple Robe

August 25, 1999

The energy in my room starts increasing early this morning. I am lying in bed, not really asleep and not really awake, watching a vision unfold inside my head.

I see myself being escorted by two beings that appear to be human; one on each side of me. We walk out from behind a curtain and across a floor, stopping at bottom center of a stage. They accompany me up the three steps onto the stage. There is a long line of beings in formal attire standing in front of us. One from the center of the line steps forward and walks over to me. He hands me a staff with an emblem mounted on top. The emblem looks like a "W" and an "M" superimposed over each other inside a circle. The staff is about twelve inches long. I think the emblem means Man and Woman united in harmony. Then, the being speaks to me and I audibly hear the words: "You are a member of the Melchizedek priesthood."

My two escorts raise a purple robe and place it on my shoulders, pull it around to the front and, as they fasten it at the neck, a profound feeling comes over me. The robe is very heavy and everything becomes still and silent. I feel separated from the rest of the world. I feel a mantle of responsibility coming down on me and I can feel the weight of that responsibility.

I am also sitting in the audience watching while this is unfolding on the stage. I notice I am the only one sitting in the audience; all the other seats are empty.

And I am up in the projection booth focusing down on me on the stage and, at the same time, I can see me sitting in the audience.

I am present in the projection booth above the auditorium, present in the audience, and present on the stage all at the same time. I am in all three separate places simultaneously and consciously aware of myself in all three places. There are three of me in the awareness of my one consciousness. I am not only the object of the initiation, I am my own two witnesses!

As the days pass, I notice other people in my life living life's daily drama, but I now have this circle of protection around me separating me from all that drama and chaos. I feel like I am living in the eye of the hurricane. From my new point of view, I have clarity of vision of what is happening to those around me and it is easy for me to step in and stand with them in strength, while remaining separate from their drama.

This experience changes my life permanently. I no longer know who I am or what I might do in any given circumstance. My emotional past is severed and, until something happens, I do not know how I will respond to it.

I received the gift of walking through life without being dragged through the chaos of it. I am very excited that life has become a new adventure for me! I am experiencing everything from a new perspective.

Cougar Hot Springs

September 1999

I have difficulty breathing, especially at night when I try to sleep, so I decide to see a specialist. I fell out of a tree as a child and broke my nose. The surgeon says I have a deviated septum so I am going to have the surgery to correct it.

After the surgery, and because of all the drugs administered during the surgery, I decide to go to Cougar Hot Springs to detox. It is a beautiful day and there are only a few people here so I disrobe and get in. Cougar Hot Springs is clothing optional and my modus operandi is to look around and see if I know anyone. If I do not know anyone, I disrobe and get in. If I know even one person, I wear shorts and a shirt. I cannot disrobe in front of anyone I know.

I am enjoying the second to the hottest tub and looking around at all the people here. There is a woman tenderly holding and comforting a man who obviously has been shot or stabbed in his side and is traumatized. There is a man drinking wine from a bottle concealed in a brown paper bag. There is the motorcyclist I passed in the canyon on my way up the mountain. And there is one man in the tub above me, the hottest tub, who is glowing! I can see his aura! He has a white glow, like a light bulb, that emanates out about eight inches from his body.

I say to myself, "Look at that, there's a wizard!" I just finished reading Merlin by Deepak Chopra so I am into wizards and magic. I look up at him and imagine what it would be like to walk in the woods with a wizard and have mystical experiences. I fantasize about life with a wizard for the rest of the afternoon as I enjoy my soak in the hot tub.

At one point the wizard stands up and walks past me to the dressing area. He is the whitest white man I have ever seen! I guess it is the glow that makes him seem so white. He sits on a rock and rolls himself a cigarette.

Cougar closes at dusk. Anyone not out by dusk will be handed a $60 violation ticket by a Forest Service law enforcement officer waiting at the exit. Everyone is out except me. I love being up here alone, especially when the sun is setting. I push dusk to the limit! I have to leave now to avoid a ticket.

At the top of the steps, a man steps out and gives me a hug. It is the wizard! I give him a courtesy hug back, which he rejects, so I give him a real hug. We proceed to walk out together and talk all the way down the path to the parking lot. He is carrying this huge piece of black basalt rock shaped like a crystal. He says he was talking with Jacob (one of the local hot spring keepers) earlier in the day and had a mystical experience that heightened his consciousness. Then Jacob ran off into the forest and came back with this rock and told him, "I don't know why, but this is for you."

As we talk I find out his name is Carlo, he is a botanist, works as a temporary for the US Forest Service, and lives west of the Wallowa-Whitman Mountains. Carlo tells me he is gathering lava stones to take to a sweat lodge community in Colorado. He is amazed that Jacob came back with this heavy stone for him. When we reach the parking lot he is met by friends, and I walk over to my car and drive home.

I am at home for a day or so when I begin to feel sick to my stomach. The kind of sick an adolescent girl feels about her first boyfriend. I question myself, "What is this? This feels like puppy love! How can this be? I do not even know this man!" A couple more days pass and I feel sicker and sicker. I think there really is no reason for this, it must be Spirit talking to me, so I say, "Ok Spirit, I will try to find him."

I look up Forest Service offices around where I live, there are three, and I check their staff listings. There is no staff member named Carlo listed. I say, "Ok, I'm done! I made an effort and I cannot find him." I am thinking I am through with this matter, but my stomach keeps telling me otherwise. I am constantly sick to my stomach. I get back on the computer and send emails to the three Forest Service offices, asking if they have a temporary employee named Carlo working in their office? One office writes back and says no and wishes me good luck in finding him. My emails to the other two offices bounce back with an "incorrect address" message. Again, I think I am done with the search.

I am so sick to my stomach the next day! I say, "Ok, I will try one more time!" Giving it much thought, I decide to open a map and see where the Wallowa-Whitman Mountains are. There on the map is the icon for the US Forest Service office in Pendleton, just west of the mountains. I click on the icon and it gives me the name and address of the supervisor.

I work for the Employment Department of the State of Oregon. I do not want to get Carlo in any trouble for receiving personal mail, so I write the letter to the supervisor as if I am trying to find permanent employment for him since he is only a temporary employee with the Forest Service.

Shortly after starting work today, an email arrives from Carlo! I stare at it for a moment in amazement; I have found the proverbial needle in the haystack!

He says he is returning to Colorado because tomorrow, September 30th, will be his last day of employment. Within a few hours he says his position has been extended until November. Then later that afternoon, he says his position has been extended to the end of the year! No wonder Spirit pressed me so hard to find this man, he was leaving the state and I needed to find him before that happened. After we make contact, we are able to spend time together and get to know each other.

We begin exchanging ideas and experiences through emails. I feel I have nothing to hide since we met in the nude! I tell him about my experience out on the Grid and with the Purple Robe. These two experiences changed my life and they had happened recently. I really am not sure who I am anymore. It is as if a part of the data base in my mind has been erased and I am starting over again.

Corresponding with Carlo makes me ask: "What do I want in a relationship? Who am I really? What principles do I stand on?" Here are some of my answers:

- Change is the only constant and life would be boring without constant change.
- Eternity is found by living in the moment and my future is unfolding before me.
- Hindsight is one of my greatest teachers.

- Acceptance and forgiveness are my allies.
- All paradoxes are true. They are simply the opposite ends of the same energy.
- All expectations are false. Once the words "I expect" come out of my mouth, it does not matter what words follow next. I have set up limits and parameters I need someone else to fill. I have robbed the "other" of freedom of expression and creativity.
- A companion without sex is only half a coin. A passionate mutually enhancing sexual relationship is the other side of the coin.
- Relationships are meant to enhance the evolution of each other's soul.
- Sometimes the only way to open a heart is to break it open.
- Anything I do from a base of love, be it togetherness or separateness, will be fruitful.

BIG BLACK BIRD

November 1999

Carlo and I decide to spend the day in the Blue Mountains. Driving up the road gives me a feeling we are entering the *Cathedral of the Forest*. The air is fresh and fragrant. We stop and admire the beauty of the trees, evergreens and yellow larch speckle the hillside.

We drive further up the mountain and stop in an area where we can take a walk. It is hunting season, but we do not have orange vests. We are careful about where we decide to walk.

A breeze comes up and the trees begin to sway. We notice this one group of trees immediately around us seems to be entertaining us. There are 4 trees, one is bouncing up and down like Miss Piggy with a tutu on, another is swaying back and forth, another is whistling as the breeze blows through its bare branches, while another is shaking its leaves like tiny tambourines making a tinkling sound. I feel like we are being serenaded by the forest! We stand here enjoying the music until the breeze stops.

We find a log and sit down. A hill with a wide fire break is directly in front of where we are sitting. We are conversing when I see a tiny black dot way up in the sky. At first I think it is one of those floaters I sometimes get in my eyes, but I keep watching as it keeps getting bigger. It moves very fast and is coming down and towards us! What seemed to be a black dot is actually a huge soaring bird! It swoops down at the top of the hill and glides over the fire break. It looks to me like it is hunting! Its wing span extends over the firebreak and over the trees on both sides. It is enormous!

As it gets closer and closer, I become alarmed and jump up! In my mind's eye, I imagine the bird feeding Carlo and I to its young in a nest, it is that big! It can pick both of us up in its talons without any problem. We are the size of mice to this bird.

When I jump up frightened, the bird stops in midair, pulls in its wings, and turns its body as if it is going to lower its feet and land but, instead, pixel by pixel it begins to disappear. As each pixel pops I can see the blue sky where the solidness of the bird's body used to be. Like bubbles popping, one at a time, faster and faster, it vanishes right before my eyes!

It must be an interdimensional bird! It was solid black, like construction paper, not reflecting any light. Carlo saw the awe on my face, but he could not see what I was seeing. He kept asking, "What do you see, what do you see?!" But it was all happening so fast I could not talk until it was over.

This evening, as we drive down the mountain heading for home, we come upon several deer standing on the side of the road looking at us. On the opposite side is a grouse looking at us. We passed hunters on our way down and these animals might get shot if they stay in plain view, so Carlo exits the car and chases them off.

Thank you Spirit for another amazing day!

The Masters Visit

December 1999

I am lying in bed comfortably when the energy in the room and in me starts increasing. I know something magical is going to happen again, so I close my eyes and wait.

In my inner vision, I see Lahiri Mahasaya rise up out of the dark and float into the background. Then Sri Yukteswar rises up out of the dark and stops in front of Lahiri Mahasaya and looks directly at me. Energy starts pouring into my body through my 3rd eye. Buzzing, buzzing, buzzing! Sri Yukteswar is filling me with energy! He not only fills me, he packs it in! Then Sri Yukteswar floats into the background.

Next, Carlo floats into view! He is sitting in lotus posture, has a big smile on his face and his head is rocking from side to side. He is wearing Levis and a green plaid shirt. He just floats through and out without stopping!

I think, "Hmmm, Carlo has been praying about me. He must have prayed to his Masters about our relationship and, when they came to give me a blessing, they brought him along."

I ask Carlo if he is consciously aware of this visit, being as he is in it, and he says, "No."

Visiting Carlo

I am on my way home from a weekend visit with Carlo in Pendleton. It is night and I am driving down the Columbia Gorge. I raise my finger to push my glasses back up my nose when the bridge breaks in half and my glasses fall in my lap. I wear glasses all the time, I am not one of those people who puts them on and takes them off, I cannot see without them.

Looking out my windshield, I can only see as far down the road as my headlights extend light, everything beyond that is total blackness. I fixate on the line down the center of the road so I can stay in my lane and I keep driving. Poles are whizzing past on my right and I do not see them coming. This startles me, I never realized how blind I am without my glasses!

I contemplate my options. I remember I have an emergency kit in my trunk that includes an old pair of prescription sunglasses. They have been in there for years, but they might be better than the predicament I am in, so I decide to stop and check.

I need to pull over to the side of the road, but I cannot see it! I have driven this gorge many times and I know there are places where there is a nice wide shoulder and where there is a narrow shoulder with a drop off towards the river. I do not know if the shoulder next to me is wide or narrow! I just have to take a chance and find out. I start counting between passing poles to see if they are equal distance apart. I pull over as soon as the next pole passes, hoping I am in a spot with a wide shoulder, and immediately stop. I do not hit anything and I do not end up in the river! What a relief!

I retrieve my old sunglasses from the trunk and put them on. They have a very dark tint and help a little but not much. I am sitting in my car, hoping if I give it a little more time my eyes will adjust to these glasses and I will be able to see better, when an 18 wheeler passes me on the road. I pull out immediately and get directly behind the truck. I follow his tail lights all the way into Portland; from there on the highway is lit and, even though I am wearing sunglasses, I can see!

February 2000

Lasik surgery is new. This Columbia Gorge experience makes me realize that if I lose or break my glasses, I will be blind and unable to help myself. So I decide to learn more about Lasik surgery.

I decide to do it! I have an appointment for the surgery. The receptionist calls me into the office and hands me the authorization papers to sign. The doctor enters and proceeds to tell me all the horrible possible outcomes that might occur, one of them becoming totally blind for the rest of my life. He repeats this scenario at least twice, and it scares me beyond belief. My heart is pounding and my breathing is erratic as I try to imagine living my life totally blind. I just cannot accept that thought! I live alone and I earn my own living. I would not be able to provide for myself if I were blind.

I decide not to have the surgery! Then I consider the other possibility; what if surgery goes well and I end up being able to see without glasses? I know if I were on a boat that capsized, and I lost my glasses, I would not be able to see the shore and know which way to swim.

I say a prayer to Lahiri Mahasaya. At one time he stated, "I will protect you if you accept me as your protector." So I pray, "Lahiri Mahasaya, I have decided not to have this surgery. I am going to get up and walk out of here unless you tell me, in some way, I will be all right. If the doctors are having a good day and will do a good job, and I will not end up blind, please let me know and I will have the surgery."

Immediately, my heart slows down and my breathing eases! I become calm and all worry leaves me. I know this is Lahiri Mahasaya's doing because I have absolutely no control over my raging fear. He dissipates my fear so I sign the paperwork. I know I will be alright!

After Lasik surgery my vision is improved but not 20/20. However, I can still see without glasses now! I lost my close vision and obtained long vision. I still wear glasses to read. Not having to wear glasses was never my objective.

So again, a Master has reached through the veil and touched my life in a very meaningful way and my life changes again from this point on.

O Sole Mio

February 2000

Last night I had the wildest dream. Carlo says I went to the astral world and was welcomed there by an Italian family.

The Dream

I am in a boat crossing a lake. When I reach the shore it is lined with private homes. All the back yards are fenced. I am looking for a way to get to the street beyond the homes. I realize I will have to pass through someone's back yard. I open a gate and enter, hoping to find another gate leading to the front yard and then the street. This house does not have a side gate, so I knock on the door and ask if I may pass through their home to get to the street. They welcome me in.

I enter and see the grandmother standing at a small table next to the kitchen door. The table is filled with sweets. The radio is on and she is singing along. Her lips are perfectly synchronizing with the song, and she makes a hand gesture towards the table offering me sweets. There are cookies and numerous small cakes. She has short white curly hair and is wearing a small printed dress with a round collar that buttons up to her neck.

I say, "No thank you" to the sweets and move into the family room in search of the front door. Standing there, in the family room, are three young men practicing guitar and singing. They are practicing a completely different song than the one the grandmother is singing. They are not very good! They keep playing flat cords and sour notes, then stop and start over again. They do not pay any attention to me; they just keep practicing.

From down the hallway, behind the guitar playing boys, I hear a man singing in the shower. It must be the father of this house. He is not very good either! He is singing O Sole Mio at full volume! This house is a cacophony of sound!

I finally find the living room and I see the front door. I can tell it is the living room because the green sofa is covered in plastic. I head for the front door when I hear a woman call out to me to wait. As I turn around to face her, she hands me a paper bag full of sweets and walks with me to the front door. She is the mother of this house.

I exit the house and, when I reach the street, I am not sure which way to go. I do not know where I am. I make a wild guess and turn left down the road hoping to find a nearby town.

In the last scene of this dream, I am standing at the edge of the lake beside the boat I arrived in. I untie the boat and I am ready to push it back into the water and return home when I look across the lake and see my "other" self. I am walking down the two lane road that borders the lake and leads to town.

This was quite an adventure. I got a taste of true Italian hospitality!

MEETING PARAMAHANSA YOGANANDA

March 6, 2000

I am going to a special service with my local group of Self Realization Fellowship (SRF) meditators tonight. This service is in honor of Paramahansa Yogananda's passing; his Mahasamadhi. There are 12 of us and it is being held in the conference room of a local office building.

The room is beautiful! It is set up with pictures, flowers and candles. The man I sit down next to hands me a red rose.

The service opens with chanting and continues into meditation. Then, there is a reading from the SRF service manual filled with beautiful words of wisdom written by the Master.

During this special service, the Master's presence draws close to his students and devotees and he blesses them. One by one we walk up to the Master's picture and kneel before it, offering our flowers as a gift of beauty and sweet fragrance.

As I watch the others kneel before the Master and silently share with him from their hearts, I wonder, "What will I say?" as this is the first time I am attending such a ceremony.

As I approach Master's picture, I decide to introduce myself. I kneel down, lay my rose before the photo with the petals facing the Master and say, "I offer you an open heart and an open mind, please teach me."

The most beautiful energy begins flowing from his picture; it flows like a river across the small table that holds his photo and our flower offerings, then surrounds me as I am kneeling. It is a very tender, compassionate, and powerful energy. Paramahansa Yogananda is omnipresent, reaching out and touching me from beyond the veil. My small heart is filled to overflowing; I am deeply touched that he knows me and acknowledges me.

Deep Roots

March 11, 2000

I wake up early, around sunrise, then fall back into the dream state and watch this visual unfold.

I am helping a friend clean and fix up an old house he is living in temporarily. While washing the bathroom floor, I bump the water line to the toilet and it begins to leak. It stops leaking when I move it back to its original position. I tell my friend not to touch that line; if its moved, it will leak.

While walking outside in front of the house, I notice plants growing out of the joints in the concrete driveway. I know these plants can crack the driveway or cause it to rise unevenly, so I feel the need to remove them. A construction worker in the vicinity tried to pull them out earlier today, but the roots remained firm. Only parts of the tops broke off.

I reach down and grasp a remaining plant top and gently pull up on it. It slips out of the ground with ease. I am amazed to see the entire root system still intact and surprised at how long the roots are and how deep they grew. I lay the plant down on the side of the driveway and go to the next one. I pull on it gently and it slips out of the ground with ease. Its root system is a little larger and deeper than the first one, but it is just as easy to remove. The last plant is woodier and probably has been growing here for a longer period of time. I reach down and jiggle it a little; it slips out of the ground with ease too.

The size of these root systems is incredible! There are multiple roots interconnected with the aerial part of the plant and, measuring them against my own body, they are the exact same size! The root system is five feet, nine inches long and the width is just a few inches shorter than the width of my shoulders.

Since I am the one who removes these roots, I have the impression that they are exactly my size, and they come out of the ground with ease, because they are core belief systems that have been deeply embedded and growing within me! I had no idea I had such large, firmly rooted belief systems that needed to be removed!

I wait patiently to find out what has changed in me because I will not know what is different until something happens and I find I no longer react to it in the same old way.

This reminds me of the story of King Arthur and his sword Excalibur. Only he could pull it out of the rock because it was his work to do.

The AUM

2000

The Self Realization Fellowship (SRF) monks are traveling around to the different meditation groups and one of their stops is Portland, Oregon. My friends Karin and Caroline arrange to go and rent a room at the hotel where the event will be hosted. I cannot afford to rent a room on my own, so they invite me to stay in their room on a rollaway cot for free.

During one afternoon session, the monks show a movie of Yogananda with his early disciples. In the movie Yogananda asks Mrinalini Mata if she will accept him as her Guru.

As I watch the movie, I see Yogananda turn and face the audience and look directly at me as he asks the question, "Will you accept me as your Guru?" I look back at him and silently reply, "If everything you say is true, yes."

Later in another scene in the movie, Yogananda says to Mrinalini Mata, "Follow my instructions and you will know God" and, if not exactly those words, then words implying that. I say to myself, "Oh, Yogananda I wish you had not said that! I heard the Catholic Church make that promise and it was a lie, and I heard the Mormon Church make that promise and it was a lie too. I really wish you had not said that! I do not want to go years and years down this path and find out it is another lie."

The movie ends and we are dismissed for the evening. We go out to eat and enjoy each other's company. Later we go back to our room and go to bed. My cot is in the kitchenette between the air conditioner and a small refrigerator. The motors on both pieces of equipment are humming and cycling on and off. After a while the hum mesmerizes me and I fall asleep.

Sometime during the night I begin vibrating with energy. I sit up and open my eyes, look around the room, but cannot see anything or anyone. I lay back down and say, "Ok, I am ready." I know something unusual is about to happen because I have felt large energy influxes like this before and something magical always happens when this type of energy arrives.

Everything goes silent all at once. I cannot hear the refrigerator. I cannot hear the air conditioner. I cannot hear my own breathing or my own heart beating anymore.

A black funnel appears above me and I begin to drift up and into it. The funnel gets wider and wider as I go higher; this funnel is filled with all-encompassing blackness and all-consuming silence. I am in total darkness and total silence. I keep rising and the edges of the funnel widen to the point where they are imperceptible to me. I keep rising and rising and then suddenly, I pop up and out into total light and sound! I am hearing the A-U-M! It sounds like a river; it flows without hesitation and without end, a constant steady stream of vibrating sound. I can hear each letter individually, the A says A, the U says U, and the M says M! I can also hear them all together in unison saying their name – AUM!

I know why I am standing here in the flow of the AUM! I expressed doubt to Yogananda during the film, and he heard me. He brought me here to prove that he is not lying. He felt the doubt in my heart and brought me here to dissolve it. I now know he teaches truth so I say, "Ok, I believe you!" and I begin descending back down the black funnel, back into my body on the bed. While the ascent took a long time, the decent was almost immediate.

As I lay on the cot, I can hear the air conditioner and the refrigerator humming and cycling on and off and I can hear my breathing and feel my heart beating again. These sounds seem much louder now after being in total silence and then the crystal clear river of AUM!

I am new to SRF. It is not until later that I learn how exceptional and special this experience really has been.

Interviewed by Masters

June 2000

It is the weekend and I am heading up to Santiam Park again today. I have my snack, chair, book, and I am looking forward to my body and mind coming to a place of balance and peace within!

I arrive at the park and there are people here today fishing in the river, a father and son. I set my chair up in the sunshine next to the river and begin to read.

Dusk is approaching and I start walking around the sport fields, like I always do, before leaving the park. The wind is blowing and rustling the leaves on the trees. I look across the field to the trees on the other side and see a huge Egyptian statue superimposed over the leaves, as if it is being projected there. The statue is the one of a pharaoh, with a woman standing next to him that only comes up to his knee.

I stop dead in my tracks and just stare at it. Then a voice says, "Do you see this statue?" I say, "Yes." The voice says, "Do you know what this statue means?" I hesitate a bit then say, "History teaches that this statue signifies the woman is less important than the man, that is why she only comes up to his knee."

I hear a murmuring, a conversation going on between three invisible masters up there in the sky. Then a voice says, "The true meaning of this statue is that the woman supports the man, that is why she comes to his knee, and the man protects the woman, that is why he looms over her."

I think about that for a few seconds and I understand what they mean. Then a voice says, "Can you do that?" I reply, "Well yes, if there is such a man." The Masters voices and the statue in the leaves vanish.

I am left standing in the park alone. I wonder if this interview has something to do with Carlo? So many mystical things have happened related to Carlo I assume this one is about him too.

The Struggle for Silence

October 29, 2000

SRF group meditation is unusually difficult for me today. We enter meditation by chanting aloud, then softer and softer until we are chanting silently within. Today I have difficulty quieting my five senses, I am restless.

I focus on my 3rd eye and see the color purple. I continue chanting silently. After a few minutes, the "judge" part of me speaks up and says, "You are supposed to be in silence, not chanting!" I "sssshhhhhh" my "chanting self" and look around inside to see if every other part of me is in silence.

I am in silence for a moment or two until I notice my "ears" perking up. I can hear every sound in the room and out on the street. I am captivated by sound! Someone is snoring, two stomachs are growling, people are swallowing their saliva, outside people are talking, cars are passing, and the overhead lights are humming. The "judge" interrupts my "listening self" and says, "You are supposed to be in silence, not listening to everything else!" So I "sssshhhhhh" my "listening self" and again seek silence.

There is silence only for a very brief time. I notice my "eyes" are not in the raised position focusing on the 3rd eye, they are looking down. Remembering what Yogananda said about keeping the eyes raised, I raise my eyes and see the "sexual/sensual" part of me. She is humming, tenderly loving and honoring her beloved! Only recently does she feel free enough to express herself uninhibited and I have no desire to "sssshhhhh" her! This part of me needs to be able to express love, not to be "sssshhhhhhed!"

So, I take my consciousness down into my heart and invite all my chanting, seeing, feeling, hearing, touching parts to join me there. My "senses" arrive along with a very wide-awake, wide-eyed, childlike part that just wants to sit and be loved.

I pray to Yogananda, "We are all too wide awake and excited to sit in silence, please come and sit with us in this noise and love in my heart!" I imagine him sitting with us under a tree, arms outstretched, as we are all encircled in his loving embrace!

He literally joins us and his energy feels soft, gently and comforting! All my parts continue to do what they want to do until they have done it enough and they begin to calm down. After a while, I notice I cannot feel my hands anymore, or my feet, or the saliva in my mouth. Silence is creeping up on us! A few minutes later the meditation is over and I drive home.

On the way home I assess my meditation. At first I feel like I have failed because I could not keep my eyes turned "up" and find silence as instructed. But then again, I finally did find silence! I found it by going "down" and allowing the inner chaos to unwind. And Yogananda did support me, he did show up and comfort me, and calm me, to the point where silence did steal over this noisy being I call me. I am very grateful for this experience.

A Visit from Hafiz

Summer 2001

Carlo is living in New Jersey and I am living in Oregon. He has been working there for about a year and a half now. We fly back and forth using our vacation time to visit each other, while he unsuccessfully applies for jobs back here in Oregon.

During the time we are apart, we read the same spiritual books and discuss them over the phone. The Gift, a book of poetry by Hafiz, is particularly impressive to me. Hafiz is in love with God and all his poems are written to God expressing his love. They are most beautiful! Hafiz's expression is very simple and direct from his heart and soul.

One night, after reading one of Hafiz's poems, I am thinking about how he writes with such simplicity and beauty and wish I could express to Carlo my love for him in such a manner. Just saying "I love you" seems empty compared to how Hafiz expresses his love. I go to bed with this thought on my mind.

Early in the morning, I wake up hearing a muffled voice in my head. Paying attention to the voice, I realize it is Hafiz! I can tell from the meter and simplicity of words that it is him! He is softy speaking to me.

I rush to my computer and begin typing what I am hearing. I read it back aloud, and in my head, I hear Hafiz correct me. I make the corrections and read it aloud to him again. Over and over I read what I have received to Hafiz and I hear his corrections. After a time Hafiz is silent, he leaves me when I finally have it right. I am very pleased!

Hafiz expresses that God is love and when you are in love you are in God!

Carlo

Thou art love in action,
A true Master Teacher.
I am thy student,
Unfolding in love with thee.
Thou hast awakened love in me.
Thou art the door and the doorman,
Through which I enter into love.
Naked and vulnerable I stand within.
I am consumed, re-fashioned in loves refining fire.
Each fire brings greater expansion,
ecstasy, bliss.
Each fire reveals another face of God.
God reaches through you, and embraces me.
I reach into you, and find God.
Thou art love.

Diane

GROUNDING

September 26, 2001

My friend Karin calls in the middle of the night. She thinks she is having a heart attack. She does not have any pain though, so I tell her it cannot be a heart attack. Heart attacks are very painful.

After she hangs up, I try to "tune" into her. I try to make a 3rd eye connection and send soothing, calming energy, but it is not working. I cannot make the connection. Next, I try a heart connection. The heart connection works, but it does not calm her down at all; all that she is feeling starts flowing into me! My energy shoots up, my heart starts skipping, palpitating, and beating in my throat! I realize she has too much electricity in her body!

I call her back and tell her she needs to ground all this electricity out of her body and not to stop trying until she succeeds!

I am now connected to this giant cloud of electricity too, so I have to get up and do a grounding exercise myself!

Abused Children

2002

I have been living alone in my apartment now for several years and many mysterious things have happened to me during this time. Several times, in the middle of the night, I am awakened by an energy increase in my surroundings.

This time, I wake up and see a child standing in my bedroom doorway glaring at me. I can see through the child so I know the child is only here in Spirit. Sometimes a boy is standing there and sometimes a girl. The oldest looks to be around 11 years old.

The children's bodies are all transparent, with some being more transparent than others. The impression I have about the degree of transparency is that, the more transparent the child is, the less life force energy the child has left for itself. The children's life force energy is being eaten away by the abusers.

No words are ever spoken. The children look at me and, from their downcast body language and the pain in their eyes, I can tell they have suffered horrific abuse. Their look says to me, "You can see what's happening to me, do something!"

My mind races around thinking, "What can I do? I do not know these children. I do not know any adult abusers. I do not know any abused children. How can I help stop this?"

I decide to send light. The only effective weapon I have against this darkness is light.

I imagine all "child-abusing thoughts" contained in one big black cloud, like a rain cloud. Using Reiki and all the energy in my being, I project it out my third eye into the cloud with the intention of dissolving the thought form of "child abuse" in all its manifestations. Energy flows, I can feel it flowing. The dark thought form is big! Even if I cannot dissolve it, I can shoot holes in it or reduce it in size. I send energy until I feel the energy waning.

Every night I send light energy to this dark "child abuse" thought form. I know the manifestation process is thought, feeling, word, then deed. If the thought is eliminated, the deed will be eliminated also. After I establish this as a regular practice, the children stop appearing in my doorway.

Why did these children come to me? Simply because I could see them. They were telling their story to strangers and I was one of those strangers.

The Golden Man

2002

I have friends who are clairvoyant, they see auras and other things. This evening while I am in bed, I say a prayer asking for "vision."

I am awakened by vibration sometime in the early morning. I open my eyes to see a golden man standing in my room. He is standing just beyond the foot of my bed facing the side wall. I have no idea why he is here.

Then, he slowly opens one eye just a tiny little bit. The light that pours out is incredible! It fills my room like a blast from a furnace and it is blinding me. I put my hands over my eyes to shield them, but the light passes right through as if no hands are there! I turn over in my bed and bury my head with my pillow, but the blinding light passes right through the pillow and the back of my head into my eyes. It is painfully bright!

I realize there is no shielding from this light, it is all penetrating! I start hollering, "Ok, ok, I see why I do not have vision. I cannot stand the light! GO AWAY GO AWAY!" and he did. He left my room and I have never asked for vision again!

My Sisters Passing

August 31, 2002

I am in New Jersey visiting Carlo this weekend. Early this morning, I watch a vision unfold inside my mind's eye.

I am sitting in the audience along with my nieces and sister. We are all sitting in the front row. Up on the stage, my sister Toots enters from the right with her purchases in hand. She pays for her items and passes through the checkout stand. She purchases a gift for each one of us and wants to present it before she leaves. It is a token of her love.

She walks off the stage and over to us. She moves from person to person, presenting each one with a necklace, expressing her love to them, saying good bye, and apologizing that she needs to leave so soon and cannot stay longer. She is very excited and in a hurry!

After placing the necklace on the last person, and concluding her conversation, she quickly returns to the stage, and exits left.

A few hours later my mother calls me on the phone and tells me Toots has passed.

The Memorial Service

September 7, 2002

The service is being held in the auditorium at the hospital where Toots worked. It is scheduled to begin at 5:30 P.M. I arrive early. I locate the auditorium, but no one is there, so I look for the hospital chapel. The chapel is quite beautiful, it is all white with a statue of Christ, an altar lit with electric candles, and a quote from the kabala on one wall. I sit down in the back and begin to center myself.

I silently chant until I reach a peaceful state, then I begin to pray. I ask for guidance from the Masters, to act in accordance with divine will. About 20 minutes into the meditation, I begin to nod and lose focus. I am not sleepy so I am very surprised that this is happening. Then, as if someone pulls on a string in the center of my head, I sit up straight, alert, and notice a ringing in my ears. Then a vibration begins to fill my body and the room. I feel as though an angelic being is in the room keeping me company! It is a beautiful experience of peace and love, so I remain here until Toots' service begins.

Toots' family, friends, and co-workers fill the auditorium. Her children each give a talk and her daughter Eileen recites a beautiful poem she wrote in honor of her mother.

For My Mom

The sun still shines, the rain still falls,
The birds sing on in the trees.
Time continues as if unaware,
That you are no longer with me.
I know you exist in a much better place,
And that you are no longer in pain,
But it seems to me astonishing still,
That all goes on just the same.
The world has changed because of my loss,
More drastically than I would have believed,
But life persists for everything here,
Is unaffected by how much I grieve.
I know in my heart that you will remain
By my side - watching over me,
And often I hear your sweet gentle voice
Still whispering, "You must believe!"
So I too survive and await the day
When we'll be together once more,

And live in the light of your undying love,
My Mother, I'll always adore.

By Eileen

Visiting Toots on the Other Side of the Veil

November 25, 2009

Several years later, in the magical dream state, I get on a bus and go visit my sister Toots in another dimension.

As the bus pulls into the parking lot, I look out the window and see a beautiful large grassy area, with a huge statue of a full racked moose standing in the center. The moose is several stories tall, including the antlers, and is facing a large building at the other end of the parking lot.

The bus stops a short distance from the building and we all get out and head toward the walkway. The children all giggly and excited run past everyone. As I enter through the doublewide glass doors, I see the children run past the counter and the clerk standing there, and out another set of doublewide glass doors into a much larger park. The children are skipping and giggling joyously down the path leading to tall leafless trees in the distance. They disappear over a small rise and out of sight. I become concerned because they are out there without any supervision.

I see silhouettes of big black birds sitting in the distant trees. They look like vultures, perched in the bare branches. As the children reappear further down the path, I see them running under those trees. The birds seem to come alive and, much to my surprise, arms appear instead of wings opening to fly! They are not birds, they are monkeys! They swing from branch to branch following the children down the path from the tree tops. My concern instantly vanishes as soon as the children and monkeys are out of sight.

The other passengers on the bus are checking in with the clerk at the desk, but I walk past them all, as if I am invisible, out into another area of the park.

I walk through a special area dedicated to small children. It is an amusement park with rides for their entertainment. Children are enjoying themselves. Each child has a guardian dressed in white watching over and accompanying them everywhere they go. I remark to one of the guardians, "There are children here too!" and the guardian replies, "Oh yes, we accompany each one who is here without a parent."

I continue walking and looking around the park. I see my sister Toots at what looks like a miniature ATM machine attached to a telephone pole. She puts something in, pulls down a lever, then greets me and tells me she is "making a payment".

She invites me over to a refreshment stand and we sit down at the counter. There are many people behind the counter dressed in uniforms of various colors and designs. If you know how to read it, the color and design of each uniform reveals the status of the person wearing it.

Toots says, "Why don't you buy something so you can see how things work around here." So I purchase a hard candy and pay with a $100 bill. The woman behind the counter gives me change in what I would call "bear money." Bear money is similar to monopoly money, only it has a picture of a bear on it. I complain and say, "This money is no good where I am going and I want my $100 bill back!" She insists the money is good and can be spent anywhere and she refuses to give me back my $100 bill! I am disgruntled, but have no choice in the matter.

Toots then asks me if I will do her a favor because she cannot do it herself while she is here in this park. I agree and she opens her purse. It is full of debris like little pieces of torn paper, shopping lists, chewing gum wrappers, and empty cigarette packaging. She takes out a huge double handful of this debris and I open my purse to receive it. As she releases the debris into my purse, it disappears! It just dissolves into thin air and is gone! Toots looks over at me and says she wants to "move out of here soon."

We walk around the park and talk for the rest of the day, enjoying each other's company. At dusk, when it is time for me to leave, we hug good bye and I exit through a turnstile. Toots remains inside the park but we can still see each other and talk to each other over the railing.

I pass through the turnstile onto a sidewalk. Between the sidewalk and the street there is a beautiful little flower bed. Sitting in the flower bed, directly in front of me, are little snow globes without any snow in them.

I pick one up and look inside and see little figurines that bounce up and down on springs. There are giraffes, elephants, tigers, bears, horses, and other animals. The unique and striking thing about this globe is that all the animals are land animals, with the exception of one - a dolphin.

Row homes are directly across the street. Looking up and down the street, it dawns on me that all the homes are in the shape of animal heads, the garages are their mouths that open and close, and the eyes are the upstairs windows that open and close. Each home is a different animal! Toots says the people living in these homes live there until they learn the lessons each animal teaches. The people are assigned to the homes according to their need. I wonder why she is not living in one of these homes, and she says there are no vacancies at the present time, they are all occupied.

I turn to Toots, we share a farewell gaze, I wave goodbye and walk down the sidewalk to the parking lot. I am on my way home.

PAIN OF SEPARATION

April 2003

I am in New Jersey visiting Carlo and it is time to return to Oregon. For some reason it is really hard to leave this time.

Carlo drives me to the airport and I cry all the way there. I cry in the boarding area and throughout the entire flight. I switch planes in Minneapolis and, when I board for the final leg of my flight, I am still crying.

The plane takes off and I am really sad. I cannot seem to reconcile my feelings. I begin thinking about Yogananda's teachings, particularly the ones about love, "Love holds the planets in their orbits and the universe is held together by the vibration of love."

I am thinking this does not match up with my present experience! If love is such a good thing, why does it hurt so much? Why would anybody want to be in love if it hurts this much?

A one inch tall Yogananda comes flying in through the fuselage of the plane and enters my heart. Then he zips out and disappears. A few moments later he comes flying back in bringing a one inch tall Carlo along with him and they both enter my heart. Then Yogananda zips out, passes through the fuselage and is gone!

The crying stops, the pain stops, and I no longer feel the separation. Yogananda put Carlo in my heart! Now, wherever I go I take him with me! Since then, I have not felt the pain of separation when we part.

November 2003

I am moving to New Jersey! We are out of vacation time and we either have to stop seeing each other or I quit my job and move to New Jersey. We have decided I am moving!

The Lake

September 26, 2006

Early this morning I have an experience in the dreamtime.

Carlo and I step off a narrow wooden dock onto a spacious tour boat that comfortably seats eight people. The boat has a palm leaf shade covering near the front, supported by four poles. We are heading out for a guided tour of a pristine ecosystem. The boat silently glides out on the water.

All of a sudden, I am seeing the scene from above, I have a bird's eye view. The boat leaves the dock and rounds a corner entering the vastness of a lake. Our guide is talking as we glide along. I expect to see oars enter the water but none do, the boat continues to glide across the surface without making a wake or a ripple. That is when I realize the boat is self-activated, as if it has its own intelligence. There is no motor or external means of propulsion.

The lake is completely still, nothing moves on its surface or within it. It is very deep in places, 60 feet or so, and crystal clear without any reflection of light or sky on its surface. The shallows are turquoise blue and the entire lake is transparent. I can see rock formations scattered across the bottom. The shadow of our boat passes over the rocks as we glide across the surface of the water. There does not seem to be anything living in this lake, there is no aquatic life visible. Inside the boat, Carlo and I are both looking down and listening to our guide's presentation.

The dream ends here and it instills in me the feelings of awe, beauty, power, depth, stillness, and quiet! My preconceived ideas are being dissolved! It leaves me with a feeling of gratitude that there could be such a place and that I could be so privileged to visit it.

The Ledge

September 30, 2006

Here is another interesting and informative experience I had during the dreamtime.

I am standing a few feet from the edge of a ledge looking down at the sea. A volcanic rock shoreline is about 15 feet below. About 20 feet over to my left, the ledge starts to give way and slip down to the shoreline. As I watch, it continues to slip away and picks up speed as it approaches me. I feel the earth begin to weaken under my feet and I step back, the landslide stops.

This part of the dream teaches me that I am the cause of any problem in my life that I think is coming from an outside source. I exert "weight" that goes out to a point of weakness and creates a reaction that "bounces" and reverberates back to me. I am the source of my own problems.

The scene in the dream changes. I see Carlo and I building a large crescent shaped wall out of stones. The purpose of this wall is to "mirror back" or return to its source, whatever its source sends out.

I see this "wall" as a point in time. Depending on how far away my wall is will determine how long it takes for whatever I send out to reverberate back to me. They say that time is speeding up. I experience this as my wall coming closer and closer to me. It does not take much time at all for what I send out to come back to me anymore. Sometimes I like it, sometimes I do not. I am living my own creation of my life. To become conscious of my own thoughts and the energy they send out, is where change begins.

If I am powerful enough to create problems, then I am powerful enough to stop problems and create something new.

Sweat Lodge Bliss

It is the year 2000 and I am attending my first sweat lodge. It is an all-women's lodge in the woods and the setting is beautiful. I am excited because I know of Carlo's great love for sweat lodges and I want to share that with him.

It is time to enter the lodge. My position in line places me in the very back of the lodge opposite the door. I sit down and, within one minute, I see dirt falling before my eyes. I am being buried alive! I panic!

I know I am in a sweat lodge and not in a cave, but I am experiencing a cave in! I see the empty fire pit in front of me and the open door. I put one foot in the fire pit and the other catapults me out the door! I cannot get out of here fast enough!

Since then, I have participated in many lodges experiencing difficulty in all of them. I hear voices saying they are going to kill me or I feel as though I cannot breathe, as if a hand is covering my nose and mouth. Sweat lodges are an experience in survival and I am always grateful, upon exiting, to have survived another one.

2006

We are attending Mystery School in New Mexico with Joseph Beautiful Painted Arrow. He brings his spiritual art work and displays it on the walls throughout the seminar. Sometimes he uses the paintings as teaching aids, explaining the deeper spiritual meaning conveyed within the picture.

Carlo and I enter the lecture hall and take our seats. Directly in front of me is a painting of a sweat lodge with an open door, steam streaming forth, snow-capped mountains in the distance, and native people lying on the green grass with a smile on their face. The caption reads, Sweat Lodge Bliss. This painting is in my direct line of vision no matter where I sit! The picture irritates me because my experience of sweat lodges is anything but blissful!

During one of the dinner breaks, I share my story with another participant. She tells me she has an appointment for a healing with Joseph at the end of the seminar and suggests I make one too. I contact Joseph and arrange for an appointment.

The seminar is over and I am sitting in the middle of the room waiting for my time to meet with Joseph. People are mulling all around talking and looking at the art work on the walls. Paintings are being taken down, sold and packaged for delivery. It is a very busy room.

My ears begin to ring, energy in the room is increasing and I can hear it. My chakras start pulsing in and out! Each one alternating direction. One bounces up and down and the next one bounces in and out. I look around the room to see who is sending this to me. No one is focused on me and Joseph is still engaged with his previous appointment. The chakra pulsing and ear ringing continue for quite some time.

A little while later Joseph calls me over for my healing. I sit down and say, "Well you already did a healing on me and I thank you very much!" He asks me to explain and I tell him about the healing I had while I was waiting to see him. He says my heart has been terrorized in a past life and he gives me a visualization exercise to practice.

Since then, I have attended many lodges. All the panic is gone, I can breathe easily, and I often find myself in a meditative state.

I am not completely over the claustrophobia I experience though. I leave the lodge if there are too many people to the point where they are touching body to body and there is no room to move. Under that circumstance I prefer to enjoy the lodge from the outside by the fire. Thank you Grandfather Joseph!

The Owl Ceremony

December 20, 2008

On my way to work, I turn the corner and see a pair of bird wings sticking straight up in the air quivering. They are laying on the shoulder of the road. I drive past, but feel compelled to go back and take a closer look.

It is a beautiful owl, decapitated, but beautiful. The head is a few inches from the body and on the road is its prey, a dead mouse. Except for the head being detached, the bird is not spoiled in any way. Its black eyes are wide open and clear. I think I arrived moments after it was decapitated.

I put the bird's body under a bush and continue on to work. I do not want anyone passing by to take the bird or even worse, run over it. The air temperature is freezing so there is no possibility of the bird decaying. My co-workers convince me to bring the bird in for identification. During my lunch hour, I try to find it but cannot. I assume it has been killed illegally and collected by the perpetrator, so I report it to U.S. Fish & Wildlife Service.

On my way home I find the bird again. I was looking in the wrong place during my lunch hour. The next morning, I take it with me to work for identification.

It is a screech owl. I call the U.S. Fish & Wildlife Service with the correct information and ask if they would like me to deliver the bird to them or give it back to Mother Nature. They say it is not an endangered bird and I can return it to nature, deliver it to them, or donate it to an educational facility for parts. The choice is up to me.

On Saturday morning, I prepare a ceremony to honor the bird and all road kill. I have seen many dead animals laying on the roadside and I want to include all of them in this ceremony. It is a very emotional experience for me and I do not know why. This will be a simple ceremony in nature, honoring nature.

I rake a circle in the leaves, under the oaks and pines in our back yard, and dig a hole in the middle for the fire. I want to honor the four elements: fire, water, earth, and air. I place a bowl of water, a rock, a razor blade, and a red cloth inside the circle. Carlo drums and chants to a soft gentle drumbeat. I place leaves and sticks in the hole and light the fire. I place the owl inside the circle. Birds from all around our woods start landing in our trees and observing the ceremony while chirping away. All the commotion catches my attention; it is as if they know what we are doing! I say prayers from my sorrowful heart for all the animals killed on the roads that I have seen in recent days and I ask permission from the bird's spirit to take the wings.

I place the bird on the rock, cut off the wings and place them in the circle. All the while tears are streaming down my face and I do not know why. I ask the bird if I may take the tail feathers as well and I am told, "No, you only asked for the wings. I want to be buried with my dignity intact." I cover the bird with the red cloth, give thanks to Mother Nature and proceed to bury the fire with the same dirt I dug out of the hole.

I take the bird wrapped in red cloth into the woods and find an undisturbed area and place the bird on the ground. I sprinkle an offering of bird seed and sunflower seeds over the entire area, and cover the bird with a piece of curled tree bark. I pray asking Mother Nature to take back her screech owl and give thanks for the gift of owl wings.

Later in the day Carlo, being sensitive to me, offers me Reiki. He feels empowered and very grounded by the Owl Ceremony. As he starts I feel our energy fields merge and flow together. Then I am energetically "squeezzzed" twice - moving out feelings of sadness from my midsection. I feel the energy step up to greater and greater vibrations. It is electrifying at one point! During this treatment I also feel a "block" go out of the right side of my back; excess "wind" go out of my left ear; a small swarm of "bees" go out of my left big toe; a "sharp" pain go out of my right knee, and an energy that feels like "water swirling" moving around my low back. It is the most awesome Reiki experience I have ever had!

The next morning, solstice Sunday, while watching the sun rise I remember an incident that happened several years ago at a workshop in Lincoln City, Oregon. During one of the meditations, I had an out-of-body experience, where my consciousness flew up to a huge wooden door covered with hieroglyphics. On the top row, the third hieroglyphic over from the left, was a carving of a bird facing forward with two curved bars over its head. I was left with the impression that this was my name, my signature.

I feel there is some connection between the bird hieroglyphic on the door and the owl with its two "curved" wings. Everything about this owl experience has felt sacred to me from the moment it started and I know not why. The amount of emotion I have felt through this has been huge.

Carlo drives to Pennsylvania to do solstice ceremony and sweat lodge with his community today. I am spending the afternoon relaxing and with eyes shut, facing the sun coming in through the window. I feel the energy of the sweat lodge come rushing in, swirling and billowing. I feel very connected to Carlo and his ceremony. I see various shades of orange and red in my mind's eye. I feel the energy come in and I know they are starting the rounds and pouring water. Then the energy wanes and I know the lodge is over.

Early Monday morning, near the end of my meditation, a huge golden brown great horned owl appears in my third eye and radiates golden beams of energy! I have the impression it is the king or over soul of owls! I acknowledge the bird and again receive beautiful flowing energy. For a few moments, I just sit and look at the bird and the bird looks back at me.

Then I hear a voice in my head say, "Thou shalt not worship false images!" and the owl immediately vanishes! My ego, reverberating out of my subconscious mind with that old Christian doctrine, interferes with this beautiful interaction! Darn!

I feel the Spirit of Owl thanked us for the ceremony we performed and I am thankful for that acknowledgement.

Dog Soldiering

2005 to 2012

To Dog Soldier is to donate one's time and service, over a four day period, in support of the Sun Moon Dance.

The Sun Moon Dance came out of Joseph Beautiful Painted Arrow's vision. The dancers fast from food and water while dancing and praying to the sacred tree in the center of the arbor. Dog Soldiers attend to all the needs required to support the dance and the dancers. They watch over the dancers night and day.

Dance fields, also called arbors, are sacred sites. The energy called in by the dance is inter-dimensional. Mystical things happen whether you are dancing, chiefing, moon mothering, sun fathering, drumming, supporting, dog soldiering, or assisting in the kitchen. Everyone is blessed by the energy and beauty of the dance.

Italy – May 2006

This year Carlo is dancing his first dance in Italy and I am here to support him and dog soldier at the same time.

During one of my night shifts, I see a candle burning across the dance field in one of the dancer's tents. I become very concerned because I cannot tell if the candle is inside or outside the tent or if it is in a glass container or just an open flame. I am worried about the dancer's tent catching fire while the dancer sleeps, so I go to investigate.

I enter the dance field and, as I approach the center of the field, next to the tree, I become very disoriented. The field is spinning! I start to lose my balance and I am afraid I might fall against the tree. I do not know if it is permissible for a dog soldier to touch the tree, so I spread my legs and squat, keeping my balance as if I were skiing, and slowly make my way over to the dancer's tent. I am close enough to see the candle is outside the tent, in a glass container, and the dancer is in no danger of kicking it over while sleeping. I am greatly relieved, mission accomplished! All I have to do now is get back to my post outside the arbor!

Slowly I turn around, still squatting, and head back across the dance field. The arbor is not only spinning, it is undulating up and down at the same time! It is very difficult to traverse! I use my legs like springs, moving one leg at a time, as the arbor undulates and spins under me.

I exit the arbor and my dog soldiering partner says, "What in the world were you doing in there?!" She could not see the dance field spinning or undulating. She could only see me walking in a very weird way. I realize what goes on inside the arbor, and what goes on outside the arbor, are two entirely different things!

Our shift is over, the relief team arrives and we return to the farm house to rest. Early in the morning I have a vision.

My inner eye opens and I am standing on the floor inside an incinerator looking up the smokestack. It is a huge incinerator made of brick. The bricks are blackened from the smoke. Up on the rim of the smokestack there is a symbol, three dots, one dot at each of the three points of an invisible isosceles triangle. Deep purple black smoke rolls up the smokestack taking the symbol away. Another symbol appears, the zodiac sign of Leo. Again, deep purple black smoke rolls up the smokestack taking the symbol away. Lastly, a swastika appears, but the arms of this swastika are backwards from what I am accustomed to seeing, and again, the deep purple black smoke rumbles up the smokestack taking the symbol away! When the smoke clears, the inside of the smokestack is crystal clear and the bricks are glistening a beautiful golden green color!

I immediately walk to the dance field thinking my vision is somehow connected to what is happening out there. When I arrive, the dancers are dancing on each other's paths. After watching for a few minutes I can see they are dancing the "flower of life" pattern, traversing each other's paths at the tree.

About two weeks after we return home from Italy, I have another vision in the dreamtime.

I am standing on a train platform looking across the tracks to another train platform. A freight train, pulling boxcars, rolls into the station and stops at that platform. The boxcar doors open and people step out dressed in their finest. Some turn to the left and some turn right and walk down the platform. The freight train pulls away and another train arrives. When the doors open the same thing happens again. Men, women and children exit the boxcars turning right and left and walking away.

Some are dressed in business suits, some of the women are wearing nylons with seams down the back of their legs, some are pushing baby prams, and some are holding their children by the hand. Everyone looks happy, healthy and well to do and they all look like they know where they are going.

I think this vision represents some of the Jewish people returning from the horrors of the holocaust. They are returning with their dignity and all fully intact.

While Carlo was dancing he also had a vision. He saw graves open and spirits rise and leave. He also saw Joseph Beautiful Painted Arrow walking toward him in a huge plowed field lined by forest.

Perhaps dancing and dog soldiering in Europe healed and released some of the spirits trapped in the trauma of WWII. Carlo's heritage is from Italy and mine is from Holland. WWII ripped though both of these countries carrying many off with it.

Pennsylvania – 2006

Carlo and I are both dog soldiering at this dance. The energy is high and it is difficult to sleep. I have a vision during one of the rest periods.

I see the dance arbor spinning out in space as if it is a galaxy of its very own. There is a thin spiral cloud swirling over it and inside the cloud are many, many dots in the shape of triangles, like I saw in Italy. The triangles are swirling down and pouring into the arbor.

I ask Joseph Beautiful Painted Arrow, what do the dots represent, what is pouring into the arbor? He says, "Abundance! Abundance is pouring into the earth now and all are being blessed." Joseph had a vision when he was dancing in Australia, at the Chiefs' Dance, of a cosmic cornucopia spilling out abundance for all.

About a week later, I have a vivid dream about an unusual sweat lodge ceremony.

The sweat lodge is in the shape of an igloo and made of stone. I am the fire keeper attending this lodge. I climb up three steps to the lodge entrance and look inside. All the participants are seated in a single row around the center fire pit and are waiting.

The inside of the stone lodge is lined with paper. I enter the lodge, close the door, light the paper on fire and climb up to exit through the smoke hole in the ceiling. I fear the hole is not big enough for me to get through. I press through the hole and, as my shoulders clear, the smoke begins to rise around me.

I fear for the safety of the people inside, so I peek through the entrance door. The fire I lit is out and the outer walls of the lodge are now radiating heat. Everyone is wrapped in a shawl, sitting in a circle around the center fire pit. I secure the door and remain outside.

This is an exceptional lodge! The stones in the fire pit as well as the stone wall of the lodge itself are both heated.

Virginia – 2009

Carlo is dancing his fourth dance and I am both supporting and dog soldering. This arbor is beautiful, surrounded by huge trees with a live tree in the center.

The dance begins and I am sitting in the support section when I feel the energy of the dance coming into me through my feet! I am buzzing! When the dancers dance, the energy is intense and, when the dancers rest, the energy wanes. I think maybe it is because I am sitting on top of a root from the live tree, so I begin moving from seat to seat within the support section to test my theory. It does not matter where I am physically, when the dancers dance, the energy is intense and, when the dancers rest, the energy in me rests too. It is an awesome experience! I am totally connected to this dance!

October – 2010

Carlo is again dancing here in Virginia and I am supporting and dog soldiering.

Before the dance begins, the Moon Mother calls all the support people together and gives instructions. She says, "If you want to pray for your dancer, pray to the tree. Do not send anything directly to the dancer. The tree is the representation of Spirit, so pray to Spirit to bless your dancer. Spirit blesses the dancers according to their needs."

During the dance, I pray to the tree for Carlo from the sincerity of my heart. When I finish my prayer, Spirit responds! I see a flash of violet light come from the tree and I feel that very loving energy enter my heart! I feel both calm and blessed, and I am grateful for the Moon Mother's teaching about praying to the tree when praying for a dancer!

Sally Perry is the Chief of this dance. She is also a Swami and gifted with vision. It is said that dancers do not often fall physically at her dances. (Falling is what dancers do when they are touched by Spirit, an epiphany so to speak). When her dancers fall, she simply catches them spiritually, before they hit the ground physically, attends to them, and takes them back to their resting place. She is a very gifted Chief.

Scotland – 2014

Carlo and I arrive in Scotland for the Sun Moon Dance and the tents are already set up. They have been busy setting up for this dance for over a week. They have a beautiful dance arbor in a lush green pasture. Carlo is here to chief the drum and I am here to dog soldier.

We are staying in a lovely apartment on the second floor until the dance begins, then we are to spend our nights in a tent near the arbor with everyone else.

All the drummers are gathered in the apartment below ours for a practice session. I am upstairs reading and I can hear the drumming going on below me. They practice for quite some time and, well into the practice, I hear a whistle blow (the dancers blow whistles made out of a turkey bone while dancing), then another, then another and another! I am surprised they are blowing whistles while practicing! At one point the whistles are louder than the drum! The drumming stops and the whistles stop at the exact same moment. They practice one more chant and then end their session, but I do not hear any whistles during this last chant.

Carlo comes up stairs and I ask, "Why were all of you blowing whistles while practicing?" He says no one down there had a whistle! They were no whistles blowing and they did not hear any whistles!

I heard whistles loud and clear, undeniably! The only thing I can surmise is dancers, in another dimension, heard the chanting and drumming and were attracted by it. They responded by dancing and blowing their whistles along with the drummers as they practiced. These are the blessings of being recognized as Beautiful Painted Arrow people!

These dances are amazing. They connect us with mystical realms and other dimensions. They create healing and peace not only within the dancer and everyone else involved in the ceremony, but to this and other worlds and dimensions as well!

Hands

April 26, 2007

Carlo and I attended Joseph Beautiful Painted Arrow's Mystery School in New Mexico last week. Joseph gives so much to so many; it would really be nice to give something of value back to him. Maybe he would like some Reiki!

It is 3:30 A.M. and I am wide awake. As I focus on Joseph, and start sending Reiki, a cloud of dirt and dust forms in my mind's eye. The cloud of dust is moving and within the cloud a bright red hand appears, then another, and finally a third hand. All the fingers are pointing in different directions and the hands form a triangle.

The hands and the dust are very familiar! I purchased some material recently to make a skirt for my upcoming Drum Dance. The red hands in the vision are the same as the red hands in the pattern on the material. The only difference being the hands on my material are individual and random, while the hands in the vision form a triangle. The background color on the material is brown, like dirt and dust.

I begin to wonder if the red hands in the vision are a reaction from Joseph saying, "Stop, stop, stop! Don't send me Reiki?" So I send him an email, explaining about the Reiki and the hands, and I ask him, "Are you telling me not to send you Reiki?"

He emails back saying, "The red hands are a premonition about your dance inspired by the pattern on your skirt material and by all means do send me Reiki whenever you want. I welcome it!"

DRUM DANCES

2007 – 2013

I was introduced to the teachings of Joseph Beautiful Painted Arrow, when I met Carlo in 1999. Joseph brought the Drum Dance, Long Dance, and the Sun Moon Dance to the people from his own visions.

The Drum Dance is about healing family lineage. The dancers dance (hop, skip, or walk) forward to a feather to clear and heal the present and future generations, and dance backward, without turning around, to clear and heal their ancestral linage.

The ceremony begins with a sweat lodge for purification on Friday afternoon. After the sweat lodge, the dancers begin their fast, from both food and water, and remain fasting until the end of the dance around mid-morning on Sunday or whenever the Chief is inspired to end the dance.

Dances take us completely out of our familiar comfort zone! We stay out in nature on the dance field and may sleep in a tent during the night. The dance begins before sunrise. There are periods of dancing and periods of rest throughout the day. The dancers dance to the beat of the drum while the drummers chant sacred songs.

Drum Dance #1 in Pennsylvania – Hunger & Thirst
June 22-24, 2007

This is my first Drum Dance and I can feel the energy here from the moment I step on the land!

We are all in the sweat lodge and it is crowded. My heart starts to express fear; it is the familiar panic attack! Cedar and Copal are put on the hot rocks as they come into the lodge so I breathe in the scent and direct it to my heart with the intention of exhaling the fear. I imagine the inhale as a hand touching and summoning the fear and escorting it out on the exhale. After a few times of doing this it dissipates. After the lodge we eat our last meal, drink our last drink, and don our dancing attire!

During the last round of dancing Friday evening, "thirst" arrives! I speak to "thirst" and say, "Welcome, I have been waiting for you! We are doing a dance for Spirit, the Spirit that made us and sustains us, so we are not going to drink until Sunday around noon. Today is Friday, we will not drink tomorrow, but we will drink the next day" and "thirst" goes away.

Saturday morning I am standing ready to begin the first dance of the day when Joseph walks by and touches my hand. He says, "I love you" and I reply, "Thank you, I love you too!" What a beautiful way to start this day!

"Hunger" arrives Saturday during the time I would normally eat breakfast. I speak to hunger and say, "Welcome, I have been waiting for you! We are doing a sacred ceremony for Spirit and we are not going to eat today. We are not going to die of starvation, we are just going to suffer a little," and "hunger" goes away.

I feel extremely weak during my rest periods, all my energy seems to leave me, my heart pounds, and my breathing is heavy. Getting up is difficult but, once I start dancing again, within two or three trips to the feather and back, my energy revives and I am just fine!

I experience an increase in my vibration during two of the rest periods. This increase does nothing for me physically; it is an emotional, spiritual elevation. I see the color in my head change and its accompanying tone rises in frequency.

"Hunger" and "thirst" show up a few more times during the dance and each time I speak to it. It withdraws and patiently waits to be satisfied at the end of the dance.

I am so pleased that "hunger" and "thirst" respond to my requests! Such cooperation from my body is uncommon and in this instance greatly appreciated!

At one point, near the end of the dance, I have a vision. I see the Eiffel Tower standing to the left of the Statue of Liberty. In front of both of them is the immigration building on Ellis Island. In front of that is a small triangular piece of land surrounded by water and covered with people, shoulder to shoulder, all shouting and cheering.

At the time I did not realize what this vision meant, but looking back on it now, I know it was my ancestors cheering and welcoming me to the awareness of their existence. My parents immigrated to the United States from Holland. I was born here so I never knew my relatives that remained in Europe. I only knew my maternal aunts, uncles, and grandfather.

The Drum Dance is the dance to heal ancestral lineage. My ancestors are aware of me and now I am aware of them. I carry within my DNA all that they have passed down to me and the work of healing I am doing reverberates back through time and lineage to heal them.

My joints are a little sore and I am tired after the dance, but I find it difficult to sleep. There is too much energy moving through my body, and I keep hearing the chants in my head over and over again.

Drum Dance #2 in Pennsylvania – Sweat Lodge Required June 2009

We enter the sweat lodge and the ceremony begins. The sweat lodge has always been an experience in survival for me because I have panic attacks. I had a vision of being buried alive in the very first lodge I ever attended. So the closeness of the people around me and the feeling that I cannot get out sometimes sets off a panic attack.

I am inside the lodge, waiting for the stones to come in, when the man behind me says to the water pourer, "Permission to leave the lodge." He crawls around me on his way out and, without hesitation, I follow him. Once outside he says to me, "Your panic set off a panic attack in me." I did not say anything to him while inside the lodge. He could just feel panic reverberating off of me.

We both sit outside and he goes back in at the beginning of the last round. The lodge ends and I am both delighted and relieved, I have escaped having to participate! I walk away and ready myself for the beginning of the dance.

The dance starts and, as I am dancing towards the feather, the closer I get to the feather, I feel a buzzing and, as I dance backwards, the buzzing dissipates. Each time I approach the feather the buzzing is more intense and it reminds me of being stung by a swarm of bees. Then I get extremely hot and begin sweating profusely. At this point, I know something out of the ordinary is happening, so I try to figure it out, and I start talking to what I imagine to be the Deities of the Dance. Are they trying to communicate with me?

I tell the Deities of the Dance to intensify the energy for a yes answer and diminish the energy for a no answer. I say to them, "I am sweating profusely. Is this because I avoided the sweat lodge?" and the stinging intensifies. I say to them, "Are you telling me it is not acceptable to participate in ceremony without first participating in a sweat lodge?" and the stinging intensifies. I say to them, "I am sorry. I will not do that again. I will either not participate or sweat first." As I approach the feather line this time it is totally silent. The stinging is gone! I feel relieved and I feel like the Deities of the Dance communicated and I understood. This round of dancing ends and we all go to our resting places and the drummers and chief leave the dance field.

At the beginning of the next round of dancing the chief calls all the dancers to the center of the field and announces, "Everyone back in the sweat lodge!" I burst into tears! I thought I had avoided the sweat lodge for this ceremony! The Deities of the Dance are testing my sincerity! I had promised to sweat before doing ceremony, but I had no idea I will have to do it NOW! I know I have to keep my word even if it means I die in the lodge. So back in the sweat lodge we all go and I sob the whole time. I feel guilty that all the dancers have to sweat again because of me. Apparently the dancers can hear me sobbing because on the way out several of them tap me on the shoulder as a gesture of comfort.

We all survive and go back out on the dance field and finish our dance.

Drum Dance #3 in Pennsylvania – Pit of Sorrows
June 2010

My friend and fellow dancer Angie is dog soldiering at this dance. She approaches me with a dance shawl that she made and asks if I would like to dance with it for a while? The shawl is beautiful and it is made of the same material as my dance skirt!

Angie says this shawl is the most powerful woman's prayer shawl she ever made and that each fringe is a prayer. The shawl is heavy with fringe! I am both honored and pleased that she offers it to me.

I am dancing back and forth to the feather and the shawl fringe is swaying with each step when I hear a sound, comparable to a train whistle, off in the distance at about 9:00 o'clock. I tune into the sound but cannot remember ever hearing a train pass by here before and I have been here many times.

We begin dancing again after a rest period and I can still hear the sound, but now it is at 10:00 o'clock, a little louder and a little closer, and it is still undiscernible.

Following each rest period, when we begin dancing again, the sound keeps moving. It moves to 11:00 o'clock then 12:00 o'clock directly in front of me, and above my feather. The sound is very clear when it reaches this position. It is women wailing!!!

Sometime back in the early 1990s I fell into a black pit of pain and sorrow and these wailers at the dance remind me of that experience.

At that time, my marriage was under great stress and it seemed to me ending it would be in our best interests. Then, for no apparent reason and all of a sudden, I just fell into this black pit of misery. I actually felt the downward motion of falling. I landed in total darkness engulfed in pain. The pain and misery of that experience was intense! It was physical as well as mental and emotional unending unquenchable insatiable pain, sorrow, and misery of the most intense nature.

Apparently, there is a black pit in some dimension where all unreconciled pain, misery and sorrow goes and, if you find yourself in that place, it considers you an addition to this pot of misery and it proceeds to consume you.

I tried to pull myself out for three days. I was totally aware of the misery I was in and I realized this is not my pain. Nothing in my life experience ever happened to me to make me feel this bad so this suffering is not mine!

I called my Rapid Eye teacher, explained what was happening to me, and made an appointment for a session. She processed me and at the end of the session she said many faces of women passed over my face on their way out. She said I was releasing pain for women who were unable to release their own pain. When the session was over, I felt immediately better but I was very tired. By the next day I was revived and completely out of that sorrowful pit.

Drum Dance #4 in Tennessee – The Ancestors September 24, 2011

The fourth place on the medicine wheel is the North, the place of the ancestors, the place of wisdom. I dedicate this dance, my 4th dance, to heal my ancestors. After all, they lived in a time of great trauma and toil.

I am dancing backwards and focusing on clearing my ancestral lineage when I see, coming out from under my feet, a flow of energy that reminds me of what I would see if I were standing in a river, looking downstream, watching the water flow over boulders and rocks. As I dance backwards the energy is flowing out from under my skirt, down my dance line towards the feather, and disappearing. I am mesmerized by what I am seeing.

I decide to make an offering to the ancestors, so I light a bit of sage and, as I dance backwards, I hold the sage behind my back as a blessing for them. I know that I carry their DNA within me. As I dance forward I place the sage in front of me as a blessing for my posterity.

The ancestral energy seems to clear and stops flowing. I am not sure the lineage is clear all the way back to the beginning so I decide to dance further back on my line to clear that lineage. At one point, I bump into the chairs at the back of the dance field and cannot dance any further back due to space limitation. I think, "How can I clear ancestral karma further back if I cannot dance further back on this dance field?"

An insight comes that I can invite the ancestors to come forward, fill in behind me, and follow me forward to the feather. As I dance forward, I wave my arms, as a gesture of invitation, for all my ancestral relations to fill up the queue behind me.

Immediately the energy begins to flow again from my first step backwards! The ancestors respond and fill my queue, they accept the healing being offered! I continue dancing in this manner until the energy stops flowing and the queue feels empty. All who want healing came forward for healing!

Now I turn my focus toward my posterity. While dancing forward, I try to connect with the future generations, with the unborn. I just cannot seem to connect with them. After a while, I realize the future is cleared by clearing the past because the "now" is a result of the past, and the future will be a result of the "now." In other words, the past has to be cleared to clear and change the future.

While dancing forward, and holding the burning sage in front of me, I invite all my living family members to come and dance forward with me (in Spirit), so they can dance backwards with me and clear their past, and thereby clear their future. I can energetically feel all my children, grandchildren, brothers, sister, cousins, and friends standing beside me on my line. We dance forward and backward together, healing all that can be healed. I see the energy from the past flowing downstream into the future from under my feet!

During the rest period, I lay on my mat under a tree and feel pulsations and vibrations running up and down my body. This is a great dance!!!

Drum Dance #5 in Pennsylvania - Mind
June 18 - 20, 2012

On the medicine wheel #5 is the place of "up above" so I dedicate this dance to connecting with my higher self, my up above. Little do I know that the up above I will connect with is my own mind and not my higher self as I imagine the "up above" to be.

My mind is active the whole dance! The quiet spaces are infrequent and far between. On the very last day of this dance, during one of the rest periods, I have a vision. I see that I have planted ideas, just like one would plant seeds, into Carlo's mind.

I know I have no right to do this, this is manipulation. I become overwrought with sorrow and regret for my actions. No one has the right to enter someone else's mind with the intent to bend it to their way of thinking.

I motion to Carlo to come over to me before the last round of drumming begins because I want to clear this energy here and now, during the dance. He comes over immediately and I put my forehead to his and suck back all the thoughts and ideas that I have planted there and wanted him to believe.

I deeply apologize to him for doing this and he assures me I did him no harm and everything is alright.

Drum Dance #7 in Pennsylvania – Releasing the Past June 20 23, 2013

This is my second Drum Dance this year, I danced in Virginia last month.

In the sweat lodge, I silently state my intention to the Deities of the Dance. "Any blessing that normally would flow to me for my participation in this ceremony, please redirect it to my son to be the 'wind at his back' to help carry him forward in his healing process. I dedicate this dance to my son."

Early in the dance, a huge wave of sadness wells up and uncontrollably comes out of me like vomit. There is so much sadness it brings tears to my eyes. I cannot relate to it or identify this sadness within myself, so I feel the Deities of Dance are honoring my request and I am releasing this for my son.

During one of the rest periods, I hear noises inside my head like a short wave radio tuning in very softly and in the distance, and I feel pressure behind my eyes. Then I develop a headache that persists on and off during the rest of the dance. I have never had a headache at any of these dances before so this is something strange and new to me.

It is Saturday afternoon and it is very hot and humid. While dancing, my heart is pounding hard, I am sweating profusely, sweat is dripping into my eyes and burning, and my "fake headache'" is pounding away. During the rest period, I go back to my mat to rest in the shade and I fall asleep.

I am awakened by strange noises and vibrations going on inside my body. I hear the drums so I know the dance has started again, but I did not hear the drum calling the dancers for another round of dancing. I consider getting up and joining the dancers but then think, "maybe I did not hear the drum call because I am not supposed to dance this round," so I lay back down on my mat and continue tuning into what is happing inside my body.

After a few minutes, I see a white ghost-like figure rise up out of my body to a sitting position. It raises its right leg and places its right wrist across its raised right knee. It then places its left arm and hand behind it and leans back on that arm for support. It is looking straight ahead at the dance field. I cannot see through the figure, it is solid white, not transparent. After a pause, it slowly turns its head and looks back at me. The figure takes a long look, then stands up, takes one step towards the dance field, and disappears into nothingness.

I feel the vibrations within when it releases but I have no thoughts, feelings, or insights about what it is or what it might represent.

At the end of the dance I share this experience with Benito and he says something has released from my ancestral line. We are all connected. Genetics and karma are passed down through the generations until someone heals (releases) them. Today that someone was me!

Egyptian Dream Jewelry

August 25, 2007

Carlo and I are going out for breakfast this morning. Our electricity is out so we have the perfect excuse!

There is a store next to the restaurant that carries gifts from around the world. We stop in just to look around. While looking at some of their jewelry, I see a pendant that catches my eye. I pick it up and my energy shoots up! It is a falcon with a tiny garnet beneath it. The attached card reads: Egyptian Dream Jewelry, Falcon, Protection, Lost Mountain. The card has a picture of the Sphinx and the Pyramids on it.

My mind races back to the experience I had out on the grid when I saw the Sphinx and the Pyramids. Then I remember the time my awareness shot out of my body, as if I were a single eye, up to a huge wooden door that had a carving of a bird on it that represents my name.

These recollections come together so I buy the pendant. When I put it on my energy shoots up, my ears start ringing, and I become dizzy. During the first hours of wearing the pendant I feel on the verge of tears, disoriented, and a little dazed. The energy seems to gather and settle in my brain. I can feel it surrounding my head. This pendent carries an energetic charge for me.

After a while the pendant energy merges with my energy and I no longer feel any extraordinary effects from it.

My Mom's Passing

August 7, 2008

My mother passes away at my sister Jean's house in Arizona today and I am blessed with the opportunity to witness it from my home here in New Jersey.

I am awake, lying in bed in the early morning hours with my eyes closed, and in my inner vision I see a whirlpool opening beneath me. A white dove appears, perches at the edge of the whirlpool, and then looks straight at me and blinks. Its blinking captures my full attention, it is not just a picture of a dove, it is alive.

I know the whirlpool is opening for mom to pass through and that she is leaving the earth plane at this time. The whirlpool is her crown chakra opening, creating the tunnel of light between the worlds that she will pass through on their way out of this world.

I am very happy to see the white dove waiting for her. The dove will escort her on her journey.

Next, I see deep footprints in the sand. They are mom's footprints and they are surprisingly deep. They are the marks she leaves here on this earth, her life's impressions that she leaves behind.

My view changes and now, above my head, I see the bottom of the whirlpool with two small feet moving up and out of sight, mom's feet. I know she is not really dying here on this earth, she is birthing into another reality; a reality where loved ones await her arrival, and will sing her name in light and welcome her home.

The vision is over, mom passes, and about 2 hours later my brother phones to tell me she has passed earlier this morning.

I believe this vision was gifted to me because of the sincerity in my heart. I wanted to be with her at her time of passing so I was gifted the opportunity to be with her on the spiritual side. It is as if a window opened and I was able to look through as a witness.

The next day, just like a bubble pops, all the sadness and grief I have been feeling dissolves.

A PHONE CALL FROM MOM

September 12, 2008

Early this morning, while moving in and out of the dream state, I hear a cell phone ring and then it magically appears in my hand. I look at the phone and see my mother's name, Alida Padmos, in big black letters on a green screen. I am stunned to say the least!

The phone rings once and I stare at mom's name on the screen, I am frozen in time. I am so stunned I do not even think to answer the phone!

My mom never owned a cell phone, the phone in her house was disconnected years ago and I do not own a cell phone that looks like the one that appeared in my hand.

I am simultaneously surprised and elated by what I am seeing, my mom's name on a cell phone read out screen! Then, just as magically as the phone appears, it disappears and I am looking into my empty hand.

I asked my mom, on many occasions, to come and visit me in my dreams after leaving this earth and she would always say, "I will if I can." I would reply, "You can and you will find out that you can when you get there so come and see me!"

My mother lived in Arizona so we had long telephone visits. I would call and say, "Mom do you want to have a cup of tea?" She would say she was making a cup and we would sit and visit for an hour or so.

For my mother to call me on a phone from the other side of the veil is a completely familiar and comfortable way for her to contact me. Needless to say I am elated to hear from her! But, next time, I will answer the phone!

INVITATION TO HER GRADUATION

June 14, 2009

My mom comes and visits me in my dreams!

In the dream state, I am walking down a hallway in an ancient building with huge white stone pillars that are open to a courtyard on one side. The building resembles the temples of ancient Greece or Rome.

As I am walking down the corridor, I hear a voice say, "Hello Diane." I turn toward the direction of the voice and see a long table set up in front of the pillars. There are people sitting at the table. I look at all the faces and do not recognize any of them, but that voice is very sweet and familiar. The person speaks again, "How are you doing?" I search all the faces until I finally see it is the woman at the end that is speaking. Her face is familiar but I cannot remember, who is she? I reply, "Very well" and finally I realize I am talking to my mom! We have quite a conversation after that.

She tells me she is graduating on July 7th and that she is 92. Mom was one month shy of her 94th birthday when she passed. She invites me to the graduation and asks me to invite my Uncle John. We say our good byes and I walk away.

After leaving the corridor, I come upon my Uncle John and tell him, "Mom is graduating on July 7, she is 92, and we are invited to the graduation!" My Uncle does not respond. I do not think he can hear me.

Looking at the numerology of the date July 7 (seven being the number of transition from one level to another and here two consecutive sevens are announced) and 92 (=11 a master number). I feel honored to be invited to mom's graduation. I think my mom is moving to another dimension where she may not be able to reach down to me anymore, so I probably will not be seeing or hearing from her again.

On July 7, I hoped to see her again in my dream state however, I did not. I believe she has advanced to another level in her evolutionary process.

SEEING INTO ANOTHER DIMENSION

October 24, 2008

The energy is very high tonight and I cannot sleep because of it. I lay in bed just listening to it and feeling it pulse through my body.

As I am laying here, I see a woman and two men come through my bedroom door. They appear as if they are a black and white film being projected onto a white cloud of fog. All three are dressed in black and they walk up to the foot of my bed and "notice" me wide awake looking at them. They stop and the woman turns to the two men behind her and speaks to them. I cannot hear her words but I can see her natural animation that all humans have when talking. The woman is dressed in a long black dress, long lace trimmed sleeves with a white cuff button and puffy shoulders. The dress has a high neckline trimmed in white lace with small white buttons down the entire bodice.

They proceed to the side of my bed, stop again, and speak to each other. They can see me so I think they are deciding to find out if I am real. The woman turns toward me, bends over and reaches out her hand. She gently reaches down to touch my stomach. Her hand passes through me; this startles her and she retracts quickly!

I do not react because I do not feel anything. At this point, I know they are in another dimension and have no substance in this 3rd dimension that I am in, so there is no reason for concern.

The woman leans over and looks into my eyes. It is as if she is saying, "Who are you and where are you?" She comes closer and closer and looks deeper and deeper into my eyes. Her face is about one inch from mine and

I just look back all the time thinking, "Yes! I see you too!" Her face touches mine and I feel nothing. She stands up, steps back, and the three of them turn and exit right through the wall near the corner in my bedroom and disappear.

It takes quite a while for all the energy generated from this encounter to calm down. Sleep is impossible when there is this much energy moving in your space and in your body. After a while the energy wanes and I fall asleep.

This corner in my bedroom points to the west and it has been a problem from the day we moved into this house. It is as if there is not enough oxygen in that corner and, as the night progresses, that "no oxygen space" seems to enlarge, sometimes engulfing me if I happen to be laying on my side facing that corner. The energy in this corner actually feels dead.

I research Vaastu and the art of Feng Shui to change the energy. I hang a beautiful wind chime from the ceiling, place a vase of artificial flowers on the nightstand (there is not enough light in the bedroom for a living plant), add a Himalayan salt lamp along with a large crystal and a picture of a Saint. All this to try and change the energy in this corner. These additions improve the energy but do not entirely alleviate the problem. There is still a space of dead energy stuck in this corner.

The next morning, after my visit by the three strangers, I ask myself, "What would Joseph Beautiful Painted Arrow say about this?"

In my head, I started talking with Joseph and telling him all the things I have done to improve the energy in that corner. I tell him about my visitors the night before. Then I hear an instant reply, as clear and audible as if he were standing next to me say, "Put a mirror in the corner." I have a very nice oak framed mirror in the closet in another room so I place that on an easel on the nightstand along with all the other objects, and direct its reflection towards the bedroom door. Since then I have not had any more visitors and the energetics in that corner have changed!

I am also very pleased that Joseph not only heard me silently talking to him, he answered me! Once we are connected to a master as a student, we remain connected until we become as they are (free), no matter how many lifetimes that takes.

SEEDING THE EARTH

February 7, 2009

Early this morning, while still in the dream state, I see books with their pages blowing back and forth in the breeze. These books are scattered all over the earth in a random fashion, yet at the same time they are evenly spaced apart. There are books as far as I can see in every direction!

I run outside to see what the books are about. What are the topics? The first one I stop and look at is so very interesting; I want to read it, so I pick it up and run to the next book. It too looks very interesting; I want to read it, so I pick it up and run to the next book. After picking up several more books and running from book to book, I realize I want to read all the books! They are all so very very interesting and informative!

I stop and look at the books I am carrying in my arms, and all the books still laying on the ground with their pages blowing back and forth in the breeze. I realize I cannot possibly read all these books. There are way too many of them! I will not live long enough to read them all.

So, I ask Spirit, "What does this mean? Why so many books to read, but there are so many I can't possibly read them all?" I hear an invisible voice say, "The earth is being seeded with new knowledge."

Golden Needles of Light

May 9, 2009

This evening's sunset is just beautiful! The sky is specked with pink and black clouds and there is a golden hue being cast all over Mother Nature. Carlo and I are standing on our front porch enjoying this spectacle! A thunderstorm is moving in.

While being filled with awe and appreciation for the beautiful display happening in our yard, I see golden drops of light falling from the sky. The drops are in the shape of pine needles, long and slender, falling like rain. They seem to come from all directions and just dissolve into the earth. I hold out my hand to try and catch a few, but there is nothing tangible there to catch.

I ask Carlo if he can see the golden needles and he says, "No." He can see everything I can see except the golden needles.

Mother nature is so beautiful!

End of a Relationship

May 29, 2010

The spiritual aspect of our relationship seems to have disappeared. Carlo and I have not been experiencing joy for quite some time now so I decide I no longer want to be in this empty relationship.

I send Carlo an email informing him I will be leaving at the end of this year when my duty to my employer is finished. He is free to move out and live on his own until then, but I plan on staying in the house. He thanks me for saying what he is unable to say and we agree.

Looking at my part in this experience I ask myself, "Am I going to take injury in this?" The answer comes up a definite NO! I have a choice in how I am going to respond and how I am going to react. I may not have a choice as to how I am going to feel, and if I feel bad, then I am just going to have to go through that bad feeling.

The one thing I need to watch for is my ego pretending to be Spirit. I can feel when that happens to me and I can feel when other people are pretending too. When I catch my ego pretending to be Spirit, all I have to do to defeat it is watch it. Ego exposes itself under scrutiny.

I decide to take a "slice of time" out of daily life and work on myself. I want to establish better health habits, put more balance in my life through exercise, and establish a firm meditation practice that sustains me. The thought of separation pulls heavy on my heart. This is a "pattern" and a thought form that brings me grief. I intend to learn all I can learn from this situation.

I love Carlo dearly and will support his personal process. At some point in life you have to just "be" what you want to become. Both he and I are looking at that opportunity now. So what is it that I want to be?

I want to be loving, kind, intelligent, supportive, connected to Spirit, contributing to society as a whole, improving myself and advancing in awareness, established in a meditation practice, joyful, strong, accepted as I am, a good housekeeper, an enjoyable companion, a best friend, a good cook, an innovative thinker, have vibrant health, complete awareness of everything around me, in communion with nature, healer of self and anyone else that wants my advice, highly organized, and a teacher to all. So that's what I will do, I will become that!

December 2010

The end of the year approaches and Carlo is very amiable towards me and it seems as if our agreed upon separation is canceled.

Engram Explodes
February 2011

In the course of a conversation, something is said that triggers a core issue in me. A feeling arises, it comes up fast and furious, and I literally explode! I see pieces of myself fly out into space like shards of broken glass!

Later on, when pieces start coming back, I discover there are pieces of my personality missing and there are new pieces in their place that I have never known before. I discover that:

- I have lost some introvertedness and acquired some extrovertedness.
- The residual of fear and panic I experience in a sweat lodge is gone.
- I no longer want to be alone, I want to be around people.
- I am able to stand in my truth and face situations calmly.
- When Spirit wants to direct me, Spirit literally "pulls" on my solar plexus.

Also, I am watching videos by Swami Nithyananda, and it seems as though he is speaking directly to me! He is imparting higher perspective wisdom and has appeared in my life at a very synchronistic time. He is teaching how to come to a point of "completion" with core issues.

This explosion permanently changes me and I am fully aware of it.

Inner Awakening Program

April 9, 2011

My introduction to Swami Nithyananda came via the internet. He posts lots of videos and the one about December 21, 2012 is a view from a different perspective. After watching it, I watch many others. His videos feel like he is talking directly to me!

I am struggling with a painful old core issue of fear and insecurity. Swami is teaching how to resolve these issues and bring them to a state of "restful awareness." Restful awareness means you no longer react emotionally, you accept what happened, and you no longer resist. It happened because it happened!

I practice his teachings daily and they work as long as I hold my focus. As soon as I lose focus, and my mind wanders back into the fear, I find myself down in the depths of misery again. This teaching in particular (below) pulls me out of the drama and trauma, and it is the one I practice the most.

> *Everything that happens outside you is illusion.*
> *Everything that happens inside you, because of what happened outside you, is illusion.*
> *The only thing real is the seer.*
> *Bring your attention back to the seer.*

Swami offers a 21-day Inner Awakening program in his ashram and I decide to go. Every night Swami gives darshan. Darshan is a blessing given to each attendee individually. One evening during darshan, I look into his eyes and I see four gold stars in each eye. I think maybe it is the overhead lights reflecting there, so I move my head to the left and he follows me with his eyes. The stars are fixed, they are not light reflections. I am surprised. The next evening there are even more stars! The third evening, I kneel before him and his eyes are full of gold stars! So many I cannot count them. I tell him what I am seeing and he gives me a hug! His eyes are so incredibly clear and beautiful, they are mesmerizing. Being in Swami's aura is accompanied by a feeling similar to pressure. When I talk to him I feel as though my voice is coming from somewhere off in a cave. He has a very powerful presence!

Restful Awareness

June 6, 2011

Early in my relationship with Carlo, I have a vision. I see that I am a slave of his in Rome, many lifetimes ago. I am young with long dark hair and he is a handsome wealthy man with a set of gold laurels on his head and owns me.

When I exploded and pieces of me flew out into space, I was able to see deeper into this vision. I understood that I was attached to Carlo and I understood why.

In that past life I was in love with Carlo but, because he owned me, I had nothing to offer him. Everything I had already belonged to him, so he had no need to ask anything of me. Slaves live in fear of being cast out as they own nothing, and have no way to obtain anything, so they would suffer greatly, possibly death, if no one took care of them or provided for them.

Being in love with Carlo again in this lifetime, brought those deeply seated feelings of insecurity to the surface. However, I did not recognize that until it exploded in my face. Insecurity is part of the "slave mentality" I brought with me into this lifetime. Being the observer and seeing where those feelings came from dissolved them. Seeing this unburdened me greatly!

In this incarnation Carlo and I are together again and, because I am a free person, I do have gifts to offer him!

I am at restful awareness with this karma now. I am no longer attached to Carlo by unresolved issues and I am no longer afraid I cannot survive without him.

From the position of the observer within myself, I repurposed my attention to assist in my own development and evolution. This is a substantially empowering feeling!

Catching Wild Horses

June 2011

I am getting ready to go to a meeting when my thoughts awaken anger in me. I can feel it down deep in my belly rolling around ruminating! As time goes by, I realize the anger is not dissipating, it is actually growing.

Several times in my past, I thought if "this" or "that" happened to me, I know exactly what I will do, I know how I will respond. Low and behold when "this" and "that" actually did happen to me, I responded in a way I never thought I would! I spontaneously did what I thought I would never do!

So I do not trust myself and I decide to stay home. I do not want to embarrass myself or anyone else by acting out from an unresolved issue of my own.

As I am sitting at the computer, I notice the anger is reaching a vibrational velocity and is actually starting to move up from the lower region of my body.

I know that this ball of energy, once it hits my brain, is going to set off multiple chemical reactions. My hearing becomes muffled or may even turn off, my eyesight goes into tunnel vision, and my head feels like a cotton ball that may explode. This disabling reaction engulfs me, and I do not want it to happen.

The energy is on the move! It is up to my midsection when I decide to try and stop it from getting any higher. In my mind's eye, I grab hold of it just below my heart and hold it out in front of me. It appears as a team of four wild horses and I am clenching the reins. I am hollering, "whoa, whoa, whoa!" as they gallop wildly in the air in front of me. The horses are pulling hard trying to get away. Just when it feels like they are going to wrest the reins from my hands, the picture bursts, like a huge bubble, dispersing energy everywhere! The horses vanish, the feeling in my midsection dissolves, and the anger is gone!

I take a deep breath; thank you Spirit, thank you Spirit! My head is clear! That energy did not reach my brain and I feel enlivened! The life force energy bound up in anger has been released back into my own system!

At this point, I am able to go to the meeting, but I decide to walk in the park and celebrate my peacefulness instead.

Journey to the Unknown

November 23, 2011

I get really discouraged, give up and sink into despair, when I work on myself and incorporate daily spiritual practices into my life and I am still unable to resolve or overcome the issue. That is how I feel right now, and during the dreamtime I have this experience.

A man comes to me and invites me to go on a journey. I am told to be at a certain "meeting place" at 9:15 A.M. ready to go, and a guide will come and escort me to the "departure town".

I head out to the meeting place early, with plenty of time to spare, and on the way I run into someone I vaguely know. She waves to me and invites me into her home. She tells me she is going on this journey too. She says she does not see any need for either of us to meet up with my guide at 9:15 A.M., because she knows the way to the departure town, and she invites me to go with her later that day. She says, "If we go with your guide, we will just have to wait around the departure town for hours before the journey begins."

We are having tea and visiting when another women stops in. The new visitor says her daughter is in the house in the departure town (there is only one house there), and she does not want her daughter to spend the night in that house. She is planning on going there to pick her up before nightfall.

In the course of this conversation, I realize the departure town is pretty much a "void" spot on a map. It is in a town that only has one house, and that house has no address, and is not located on any street. So you have to know exactly where it is or you cannot find it. I become very nervous and anxious at this prospect and fearful of being late and missing my guide. I look down at my watch to discover I have forgotten it. I have no idea what time it is, so I ask my friend and she says, "9:05 A.M." My friend invites me again to go with her to the house in the departure town later on that day, and assures me we will be on time for the journey. Being as nervous and anxious as I am, I decide I still have time to meet my guide so I leave immediately for the meeting place.

My guide and I arrive at the house in the departure town, and I realize the departure time is different for each person and 9:15 A.M. is my departure time! I also realize my guide is the only person I can identify with or talk to on this journey!

We are preparing for the journey and I hear a voice say, "It is expeditious to Cross the Great Waters." I recognize this voice as the voice of the I Ching Masters telling me everything will be ok; that I am capable of making the necessary decisions and taking the journey, and I am capable of surmounting all the dangers involved.

The journey is an expedition over a high mountain pass. We have ropes, hooks, boots with ice spikes on the soles, pick axes, and other high mountain climbing gear. We follow a very narrow winding trail over a steep ice and snow covered pass. We camp along the way and travel for days.

Upon reaching the crest of the mountain we see a light in front of us. A small party of men wearing hats with head lanterns addresses our expedition by our code name, and our leader verifies that is who we are. Our leader then addresses the small party of men by their code name, and they verify that is who they are. The small party of men state they are here to guide us down the mountain and ask how many porters we have with us. Our leader says, "1,300 porters to support this expedition." I am amazed! I only see the 4 or 5 people that are standing around me and never see any porters at all! However, every time we need something, it is always there.

We follow the small party of men down the mountain to their campsite. The rest of their party is inside a huge white tent, socializing. We enter and are assimilated into their group. Hot beverages and food are being served. Everyone is friendly and welcoming. Their camp consists of about 300 persons.

What this experience did for me is take me out of the low vibrating "I do not want to live on this planet anymore" mentality, and leave me on a higher plane. The big tent and campsite are located part way down the mountain, not at the bottom. It is a temporary place, it is a resting and renewal place where I am accepted and befriended.

This dream-experience shows me the Masters hear my prayers, see my dilemma, understand I cannot get out of where I am by myself, and decide to step in and help me.

Afterthought:

The friend who invited me to travel to the "departure town" at a later time of day was merely a temptation to test my sincerity and my desire to resolve this core issue. Had I been dissuaded by her, I would have missed this opportunity.

The Final Piece
June 2014

The one missing piece to resolving this whole core issue for me is trust. I do not trust that things are working out for my highest good, and I do not trust that new doors and opportunities will open for me in the future. I tend to look at what I need to eliminate, my attachments that no longer serve me, as a loss instead of trusting that Spirit has something new for me and I need to make room to receive it.

I make an appointment with a spiritual counselor for guidance and understanding and I am told to "relax my resistance!" So I do. Instead of resisting my fears, I simply let them arise, observe them from my core, the position of the witness, and allow them to unwind and dissipate. My own fear thought forms that imprison me are dissolving!

I become more and more peaceful and more and more centered as time passes. I trust that, if I go with the flow, Spirit will take care of me in unforeseen ways and I need not concern myself with security issues anymore. I will tell the end of this story with a metaphor.

There is an employee working under, what he considers to be, an oppressive condition. The employee complains to the employer and the employer says, "This is the way it is around here, adjust to it." Being in fear of being unemployed, the employee stays at his job, tries to accept the condition, but suffers unhappily for a long time.

Then with help from a mentor, who sees things from a higher perspective, the employee loses his fear of being unemployed and goes in and tells the employer he has decided to resign rather than continue to work under the oppressive condition and gives notice. The employer does not see the condition as oppressive, because it does not oppress him. The employer has no choice but to accept the resignation.

The employer considers the situation. He looks at the condition that oppresses the employee and decides, how much of a loss will the company suffer if I remove that condition? If the loss is too great, the employee proceeds to terminate his employment. If the loss can be assimilated the employee remains with a happier healthier attitude. Either way, the employer and the employee both win because the employee resolves the resistance and fear within himself, and the employer upholds company policy. Both are free from restrictions.

This is the final piece that set me free. My Fear has been replaced with Trust. I now trust that everything that ever happened to me happened so I could evolve. The painful experiences were breaking me off from beliefs that kept me from moving forward.

I feel like I am on my sixth life in this lifetime. I have been five different people before becoming the person I am today! The person I am today is much freer and happier than the persons I used to be.

THE HEALING

2011

One of our Elders maintains an email prayer list of all the people willing to pray, send Reiki, or healing energy in the modality of their choice, to those who request it.

An email arrives requesting prayers for a toddler. The toddler is in the hospital Intensive Care Unit with a massive infection. With the email still open on my computer, directly in front of me, I send long distance Reiki to the child.

It feels like the child is too weak to overcome the infection; there is not enough life force energy left in the child to fortify with Reiki. It feels as if the infection is systemic and taking over the child's body.

I stop sending Reiki and ask, "What can I do? The child is dying!" I get a "flash of insight" that says, "Reiki the infection!" Sending Reiki to an infection is the opposite of what I do, I have always sent Reiki to give and not take away. I decide to try it knowing the child I am sending Reiki to is too weak to overcome the infection.

I start sending Reiki and I can feel the infection receiving it, taking it all in, becoming larger and larger! In my mind's eye, I can see the infection smiling at me and saying, "Thank you for strengthening me!" When the infection is as big and strong as it can get, I keep sending Reiki, and keep sending Reiki until, all of a sudden, I see the infection explode! Boom! It morphs! It is no longer an infection because Reiki changed its vibration!

A moment later, this morphed infection comes rushing through the electrical system of my computer and out the screen straight at me! I have tricked it and it is angry!

At the exact same moment, from behind my head, a ball of energy rushes past my ear into the computer screen and slams into that morphed energy. Like two waves crashing into each other from opposing directions, they surge up, splay out, and dissipate!

Shortly after that, we start receiving email updates on the child's condition. He is out of intensive care, he is able to move its hands again, he is eating, and finally, he is going home!

There are a lot of people on this email prayer list, and most likely all of them responded to this prayer request! It is wonderful to be a part of it! Thank you Reiki Masters!

Years ago I worked for the phone company as an operator. I picked up a call from a Toll Station up in the mountains one night. The man asked me a question and as I was answering him I saw an anomaly appear above my switchboard. An anomaly appears like heat waves coming off a hot road. It is invisible but yet you can see it. Then the anomaly disappeared and the man at the toll station started saying, "I just saw you! I saw you, I saw you. I can't believe it!" and he hung up. I tried ringing him back because I was worried about him. It was snowing up in the mountains and he didn't place his call. He just hung up and wandered off.

I know from experience that nonphysical energy carries awareness and can travel. When I sent Reiki to the infection, it followed the Reiki energy back to me. When I spoke with the man in the Toll Station, he was drawn by my voice and saw me. When he realized what happened, it so amazed him, he forgot all about placing his phone call!

THE CORN LADY

October 2012

Carlo is dancing with his teacher Benito in Yucca Valley this year. I plan on visiting my son and daughter-in-law in Santa Monica during that time.

We arrive on the dance grounds Thursday afternoon, and Valerie Eagle Heart invites me to spend the night. I will leave before the dance starts tomorrow. We spend time visiting and sharing experiences with everyone there. Dancers continue to arrive throughout the day. We spent the night on cots, set up in the communal eating space adjacent to the house. When morning arrives, I feel like I have been awake all night long!

In the dreamtime, I am out in the back yard with all the dancers. They are sitting in a circle around Benito. He is teaching and instructing them and I am holding a bowl of yellow corn meal on my lap.

All the dancers are quiet and attentive. Benito is sharing sacred teachings and I am observing. The teachings flow through the top of their head, down through their body, and ground into the earth.

From my position as observer, I can see the teachings as they move through the dancers. If a teaching gets stuck, I can see that too.

If it gets stuck in their head, I toss a little corn meal on their head to open their mind to higher wisdom and release earthly attachments. If it gets stuck in their chest, I toss a little corn meal on their chest to open their heart to love and release grief. If it gets stuck in their stomach, I toss a little corn meal on their stomach to open their will power and release shame. If it gets stuck in their knees, I toss a little corn meal on their knees to allow surrender and release stubbornness. And if it gets stuck in their feet, I toss a little corn meal on their feet to open their soles so they can ground all they are learning.

All night long, I watch the dancers and toss corn meal on them when and where needed, opening the way for them to receive the fullness of the teachings.

After a while, I realize I have used up a lot of corn meal and begin to wonder if there is enough left for the dance? Shortly after that thought, I wake up. Valerie asks if anyone had any dreams and I share my dreamtime experience with those that are there that morning.

The morning passes and it is time for me to leave, so I fill my pockets with corn meal and sprinkle a little on everyone's feet as I say good bye. It just seems like the appropriate thing for me to do!

After the dance, Carlo tells me about John, a dancer who knows Joseph Beautiful Painted Arrow and talks with him regularly. John arrived the morning after I left.

Carlo and John are conversing and at the end of their conversation, Carlo says to John, "Oh by the way, the corn lady gave you the corn." John lowers his head and says, "You won't believe this, but when I left Joseph to come here, Joseph told me "you will meet a lady there that will give you corn." When Joseph said that, I thought to myself, "What is he talking about?!?"

An Energetic Reading

December 14, 2012

I meet Dr. Cathy today, my friend Mary has introduced me to her. Whenever someone new enters her circle, she gets to knows them by reading their energy signature.

She says, "I am a puzzle." She follows my energy back, then it stops, and a new energy starts. It is as if I have six people in me and this puzzles her?

I experience these energetic changes as a "morphing" or "abandoning" of the old me. I move to a new vibrational level, a quantum leap so to speak. My energy signature permanently changes from that point on. Her reading makes perfect sense to me!

I liken my body to computer hardware, and my mental and emotional systems to the software. Whenever I want to change my interactions with the outside world, all I need to do is download new software. When new ideas and concepts come into my awareness, I practice them over and over, until they become my own, my very nature.

In 1986, when I began learning about new concepts and ideas, I realized I could not remember them just by reading them once or twice. I wanted to imbed them into my mind. I started making my own flash cards and, when I got stuck waiting somewhere, like in line at the grocery store or at the car wash, I would take my pile of cards out and read them. I read them over and over, until they became part of my subconscious memory. Then they began to manifest out in my life. Here is an example of one of my cards:

All things related to the same thing are equal to each other.

This saying freed me from my inferiority complex. If all things (people) are related to the same thing (God) then all things (people) are equal to each other.

- Inferiority dissolved in me.
- Hierarchy dissolved in me.
- Fear of authority dissolved in me.
- Worship or fear of someone superior dissolved in me.
- The ability to acknowledge who I am, what I think and feel, begins to arise in me.

It is a very freeing experience to comprehend, manifest, and live this principle in my daily life!

Swami and the Bird

August 5, 2013

I have been wondering how Swami Nithyananda feels, or what he might say, if he knew I am participating in Beautiful Painted Arrow ceremonies. I wonder if he still considers me part of his Sangha (spiritual community).

Last night, while in the dream state, Nithyananda appears. He just pops into my dream! He is smiling, then he blinks his eyes. The blinking captures my attention immediately! The very next instant I see him with a bird in his mouth, feathers and all! The bird is alive, and the tail end of the bird is sticking out of his mouth. Nithyananda opens his mouth a little wider, taps the tail of the bird with the palm of his hand, and in one gulp swallows the bird whole! Then poof, Nithyananda is gone out of my dream!

I am left wondering what does this mean? I know it is a metaphor, but what does it mean?

Several weeks pass and I finally understand the meaning of this metaphor. The bird represents Birdsong! Birdsong is the name of the Peace Chamber where I do most of my Beautiful Painted Arrow dances.

Swami swallowing the bird alive means Birdsong Peace Chamber is alive in him! He embodies the spiritual work I do there. He answers my question, I am still part of his Sangha!

Light Patterns

1999 to Present time

I experience "light patterns" inside my head. A burst of light, like a flash bulb goes off in my brain. A pattern appears and absorbs that light, then fades away.

The patterns change. I have only seen the same pattern twice. They are beautiful, intricate, and mathematically precise. I have seen spider web, honeycomb, concentric circles like bulls eyes on a target, concentric rectangles and crosses, crystals, pointed shards like glass exploding, and many others.

Is this an aneurism, or some other brain disorder? I wait after each episode to see what will happen, but nothing detrimental ever happens! Sometimes I feel a displacement of space inside my head, or hear a popping sound. I am always surprised there is no ill effect! It just happens and then it is over.

One time in 2005, what looks like a circular saw blade enters my head. It comes forcefully, with a loud thud, and reminds me of something in a 007 movie. It also hurt and that scares me.

I receive an email from a healing center up in New York state. Max, the Mayan crystal skull, is going to be there. I make an appointment for a half-hour healing session with Max and drive up.

Now, I am in a room alone with Max. The crystal skull is sitting on a table in front of me and I have my hands on its head. All I feel is love coming from Max! It is an energetic buzzing feeling of love and it fills me.

I talk to Max and tell him about the light flashes in my head. When I get to the part about the circular saw blade, all the energy coming out of Max changes. It snaps into action! I feel an invisible finger touching my forehead. I hear and feel something blow past my right ear, like blowing out a candle. Then the sweet energy of love begins to flow from Max again. Soon, there is a knock on the door and my time is over.

Joann Parks, Max's guardian here in the physical, is selling little skulls energized by Max. The little skulls are displayed on a table along with Max and are made of various gem stones. I buy one made of lapis lazuli and head for home.

Joann told everyone to name the little skull they bought. I want a name that will connect my little skull to Max because they have been together for a long time. I cannot think of any name that is appropriate or acceptable! While driving down the turnpike, inside my head, I hear a voice say, "My name is 'Maxine' because you and I have both seen Max!" Aha, my little skull named itself! And it is a very appropriate name indeed!

Since my visit with Max, I have had very few light flashes and, the ones I have had, have all been gentle; no loud explosions, and no displacement of energy. The last one I saw was a dandelion in the seeding stage; a puff ball of white fuzz waiting for the wind to carry it away.

Blue Light Burst
October 2, 2013

While falling asleep tonight, a burst of cobalt blue light, similar to a fire cracker, explodes in my forehead. The explosion is audibly loud, but it does not displace any "space" as events like this have in the past. This is the first time I am seeing any of these patterns in color. All of the other patterns lit up with white light.

Synchronicities

November 1, 2014

Spirit speaks to us through synchronicities. Realizing this, I pay attention to the ones that occur in my life – one happened yesterday.

My brother Mike passed away on October 1. Like my mother and I, my brother and I had a telephone relationship. He lived in Montana and I live in New Jersey. Our telephone visits were easy and enjoyable.

My father passed away many years ago on Halloween, October 31. My father and my brother have the same name, Michael Padmos. My brother and my father were very close. Mike was the first born son and the apple of my father's eye.

The synchronicity is this: In one of my telephone conversations with my brother, I told him about the phone call I received from mom after her passing, and he said he wished he had received a phone call from her. In another conversation, I told him that every Halloween I looked for dad. I always hoped dad would come visit me on that day, the day of his passing.

Yesterday was Halloween, the anniversary of my father's death, and my cell phone rang and the name on the dial was Michael Padmos! It was my brother's wife calling to inform me about the details of his Memorial Service, but none the less, it was very synchronistic that she would call me on Halloween, the day my dad passed and a month after my brother's passing!

It feels like my brother sent me a good bye message via the telephone just like my mother did. His name appeared on the dial, and he did it on the day he knew I would be looking for a message! I also have the feeling it was an expression of his great joy at being reunited with dad once again.

WEDDING CEREMONY

January 25, 2015

Carlo and I are joining hearts and hands in the sacred ceremony of marriage today! We lovingly vow to uphold and support each other's spiritual growth, upliftment and evolution! He and I are deeply touched by the power and simple beauty of this sacred gathering.

A portal of energy opens as we begin and the room fills with family from other dimensions. Dr. Cathy announces that Carlo's spiritual tribe is here in full regalia to celebrate with us. This is a very special moment! All of us present can feel it. Carlo shed's his tears and enters an altered state.

Standing with us is a small gathering of personal friends we consider family. Ben and Marie are our witnesses, Mary our beautiful hostess is offering her heart and her home, and Dr. Cathy is officiating.

Dr. Cathy has created a special ceremony for us with help from our spiritual guides, blending in our vows inspired by a wedding ceremony performed by Paramahansa Yogananda at the Mother Center. The inspiration for our ceremony came to her in blocks of information. She solemnizes our commitments and we are so very blessed to be in this circle of family and friends!

The Mind and Spiritual Intervention

We have come to understand that it is important to know how our mind works in order to release old programs that no longer serve us.

I know there is a lot of information on this subject already out there, but here is a simple explanation, hoping it will clarify how the separate parts of our mind work together, and affect the whole of our being.

By Diane Stephenson
June 30, 2013

The human being has a physical, etheric, emotional, mental and spiritual body. These bodies interpenetrate each other, with the spiritual body being separate and at the same time encompassing and interpenetrating the others.

PHYSICAL BODY – Is the one we see in the mirror and interact with on a daily basis. The physical body's state of health is a reflection of the health or clarity of the other four bodies.

ETHERIC BODY – Encompasses the physical, and receives and distributes energy from the cosmos into the physical, keeping all the cells alive. Meditation clears obstructions to the energy flowing through the etheric body. Sri Karunamayi states that chanting the Sarasvati Mantra on a daily basis purifies the etheric body.

EMOTIONAL BODY – Encompasses the etheric and the physical and, when active, causes feelings of pleasure or distress experienced in the physical. The emotional body is reactive; it reacts to thoughts from the mental body.

Emotions are "energy-in-motion" and they flow just like water flows. Emotional energy needs to flow freely, both good and bad, in order to remain healthy.

When a dam is erected in a river, the river backs up, causing pressure against the dam. In the same way, erecting an emotional dam in our body or refusing to feel our own emotions causes stress and illness in the body over time.

It is our natural state to feel everything, both the good and the bad. When experiencing an unpleasant emotion just watch it. Become the observer and watch the emotion and, in time, it will dissipate. Let's not allow the mind to engage it and spur us to react to it.

MENTAL BODY – Encompasses the emotional, etheric and physical bodies, and is the emanation of the conscious and sub-conscious mind.

Conscious mind

- Is manifest only during wakefulness.
- It keeps in touch with the exterior world through sensations and perceptions carried over the five senses of touch, taste, sight, smell, and hearing.
- Becomes fossilized without training or introspective creative thinking.

Sub-conscious mind

- Is always awake, operating the involuntary organs during sleep and memorizing conscious experiences during wakefulness.
- Runs things in the background or in the "dark" out of the awareness of the "light" of the conscious mind.
- Takes charge when the conscious mind is not paying attention, like driving the car when the conscious mind is busy rehearsing a speech or planning a meeting.

- Works like a tape recorder and repeats back to us what the conscious mind has "dropped into it" via self-talk, movies, abuse, and so on. If in the past we looked in the mirror and said to our reflection "you are ugly" the sub-conscious mind will repeat that back to us every time we look in the mirror until we change that tape. When we catch our sub-conscious mind repeating verbal abuse to us, intervene, stop that tape and replace it with a smile and a feeling of self-acceptance. Affirmations work on this level, they reprogram the sub-conscious mind.
- Descends into the nervous system and muscles and becomes the conscious state.
- Left untrained it loses its powers of recall and becomes forgetful.
- Remains hidden below the conscious mind.

SPIRITUAL BODY – Permeates all four lower bodies and is directly connected to super-consciousness.

Super-consciousness

- Experienced during deep meditation and is semi-superconscious during deep sleep.
- Is the pure intuitive, all-seeing, ever-new blissful consciousness of the soul.
- Knows everything that goes in the sub-consciousness and consciousness.
- Remembers all experiences including previous lifetimes.
- Remains hidden below the subconscious mind.

Super-consciousness is the part of our spirit that is directly connected to Creator, is ever present, and is the avenue through which spiritual intervention and intuition travels.

The spiritual part of us is the "observer." The observer lives in the "present moment" or in the "now." The observer is the only part of us that is real. The mind holds our memories of the past that no longer exist (are not real) and projections of the future that may never exist (are not real).

The way to find and strengthen our connection to the spiritual part of our self is to practice being the observer, practice bringing our attention back to the "seer," practice paying attention or focusing our consciousness, our "light," on what we are doing in the present moment.

Great ideas, insights, inspirations, and visions come out of the unexpected and are dropped into the conscious mind (descending light) via our superconscious mind. What to do or not to do is then up to us, according to our free will. Spiritual intervention can calm and quiet the mind, ease and cease the emotions, and change the physical body in an instant.

Spiritual intervention happens when law is fulfilled or when we touch the heart of Spirit. Everything material exists because it vibrates at a constant frequency that holds it in that particular form. Love vibrates at the highest frequency. If we raise the frequency of anything, we change its form. On a scale of 1 to 10, let's say water vibrates at a 5. If we lower its frequency to zero, it becomes ice. If we raise its frequency to 10, it becomes mist or steam. It is still H_2O however, its form has changed. The principle of vibration applies to thoughts and emotions as well. Sadness goes away with an infusion of energy. Sadness is a low vibration; any increase in vibration takes us out of sadness. Depressing thoughts can also be replaced with thoughts of love and appreciation for something we care about, like a pet or beauty in nature.

Synchronicities are evidence that the universe or Creator is active in our life, responding to our needs. When we have need of something and seek it from a positive loving (high vibrational) attitude, the universe conspires to make that happen through synchronicities. Events and occurrences line up, gears seemingly turn, and everything falls into place. Something happens that originally appeared as though it would not happen or it is an utter surprise. Acknowledge the synchronicities in life when they happen. Let's take a minute and simply say from our heart, "Thank you Spirit." Gratitude begets more to be grateful for.

SUMMARY – The spirit in us is our connection to power, power to manifest in our inner and outer worlds!

Our spirit is who we really are. It is the real us, the authentic us, the eternal us, the part that steps out of the body when the body dies. To experience this life from our spiritual part, is to live life as the "observer." Living life as the observer is "bringing heaven (the spiritual part of us) here on earth."

When we live our life as the observer, we have the freedom to choose which aspects of life we wish to engage in. We are no longer ensnared in the drama that goes on in or all around us. We are no longer whipped around or overcome by overwhelming thoughts and emotions. This does not mean we no longer feel emotions, it means we feel everything; our emotions are allowed to flow without obstruction and without holding onto (damming) them. We experience life fully!

Let's practice becoming the observer and watch our life change! Feelings of insecurity disappear, fears disappear, mind chatter decreases or ceases, inner peace manifests; we becomes aware of the incredible beauty all around us. Life becomes ever new and ever renewing, new people enter our circle of friends, relationships deepen, physical health improves, new ideas and inspirations flow into our conscious mind, and many other blessings manifest in our life all out of the unexpected!

AFTERWARD

I have wondered how and why these inter-dimensional and dreamtime experiences happen and I believe the answer is that Spirit responds to the "sincerity of the heart" and "purity of intention."

The most efficient way to learn anything is by experience. Spirit gives us the experience when a truth is needed to enhance our life's evolution, and we wonder, contemplate or sit with that inquiry. That experience may be in the dreamtime, or come by way of a vision, or just a knowingness that lands in our mind. The experience comes as a complete and total package of information.

Spirit talks to us through our heart and ego talks to us through our head. As long as we are in our head trying to figure it out, Spirit remains silent. When we are in our head, we can come to some marvelous conclusions and theories, but we will not really "know" because thinking about something is not the same as experiencing it.

A way to practice getting out of our head and into our heart is to take the conclusions derived in the mind down to the heart and ask the heart, "How does this feel?" Then let's sit and wait for a feeling to arise. If it feels good it is a confirmation. Spirit responds to the sincerity of the heart!

About the Author

Diane Stephenson is a truth seeker. Masters of truth and the teacher within have responded to questions held within the sincerity of her heart and provided experiences whereby she came to know the truth.

Interdimensional Dancing is a collection of spiritual experiences that illustrate this evolutionary process of personal growth. Diane lives with her husband in the pinelands in Estell Manor, New Jersey.